Christmas Gifts

FOR
Everyone

Christmas Gifts for Everyone

Edited by
Barbara Fimbel

Rodale Press, Inc.
Emmaus, Pennsylvania

A FRIEDMAN GROUP BOOK

Published in 1995 by Rodale Press, Inc.

The editors who compiled this book have tried to make all of the contents as accurate and as correct as possible. Illustrations, photographs, and text have all been carefully checked and cross-checked. However, due to the variability of materials, personal skill, and so on, neither the editors nor Rodale Press assumes any responsibility for any injuries suffered or for damages or other losses incurred that result from the material presented herein. All instructions should be carefully studied and clearly understood before beginning a project.

The editors at Rodale Press hope you will join with us in preserving nature's beauty so that others may share in the enjoyment of nature crafting. Unless you are certain that the plants or plant materials you are collecting—including leaves, stems, bark, flowers, fruits, seeds, or roots—are very common in your area, or over a wide geographic area, please do not collect them. Do not disturb or collect any plants or plant materials from parks, natural areas, or private lands without the permission of the owner. To the best of our knowledge, the plants and plant materials recommended in this book are common natural materials that can be grown and collected without harm to the environment.

Printed in the United States of America

Library of Congress Cataloging-in-Publication Data

Christmas gifts for everyone / edited by Barbara Fimbel.
    p.   cm.
    "A Friedman Group book"—T.p. verso.
    ISBN 0–87596–659–4 paperback (alk. paper)
    1. Handicraft. 2. Gifts. 3. Christmas. I. Fimbel, Barbara.
TT157.C474 1995
745.5—dc20   95–9489

Distributed in the book trade by St. Martin's Press

2 4 6 8 10 9 7 5 3 1 paperback

If you have any questions or comments concerning this book, please write to:
    Rodale Press, Inc.
    Book Readers' Service
    33 East Minor Street
    Emmaus, PA 18098

CHRISTMAS GIFTS FOR EVERYONE was prepared and produced by
    Michael Friedman Publishing Group, Inc.
    15 West 26th Street
    New York, New York 10010

Michael Friedman Publishing Group Editorial Staff:
Project Editor: Barbara Fimbel
Technical Editor: Kathleen Berlew
Instructions Editor: Charlotte J. Biro
Copy Editor: Loretta Mowat
Editorial Director: Sharyn Rosart
Designer: Andrea Karman
Layout: Robbi J. Oppermann
Illustrator: Barbara Hennig
Art Director: Jeff Batzli
Photographer: James Kozyra
Photo Stylists: Lynn McMahill and Sharon Ryan
Photography Director: Christopher C. Bain

Rodale Press Editorial Staff:
Editor: Karen Bolesta
Cover Designer: Lisa Palmer
Interior Layout: Robin M. Hepler
Illustrator: Glenn Hughes (Stitch diagrams on pp. 87, 115, 161)
Copy Editor: Maria Kasprenski Zator
Manufacturing Coordinator: Melinda B. Rizzo
Editorial Director, Home and Garden: Margaret Lydic Balitas
Senior Editor, Craft Books: Cheryl Winters Tetreau
Art Director, Home and Garden: Michael Mandarano
Copy Director, Home and Garden: Dolores Plikaitis
Editor-in-Chief, Rodale Books: William Gottlieb

Contributors
Julia Bernstein
Amy Albert Bloom
Jack Champlin
Michelle Filon
Barbara Fimbel
David Galt
Dale Joe
Patricia Richards
Lynne Shipp
Jacquelyn Smyth
Marinda Stewart

CONTENTS

Gifts for Friends

Secret Santa Gifts

Gifts for VIPs

Favor-ite Gifts

INTRODUCTION

A handmade gift is like a hug. It wraps the recipient in a moment of affection—a moment that can be recalled with pleasure over and over, bringing on a smile each time. Like that loving squeeze, a handmade remembrance contains a little bit of yourself. Your fondness, concern, and warm thoughts become a part of the finished product as surely as the time spent making it. At Christmas, we express our feelings for all of those around us—for our family, for our friends and neighbors, for people who make our lives easier during the year, and for people who can use our helping hand.

As you flip through the pages of *Christmas Gifts for Everyone*, you will come across projects selected and created for people in each group. We've given a lot of thought to these suggestions; we think these gifts will be ideally suited to those on your list. Many of the projects would be appropriate for other situations as well. Your baby-sitter, for example, might not be a teenager, but a retired schoolteacher who would prefer a lap robe or an evening bag. Your sitter might even be a young man who would be pleased by a video game rack.

While the collection of remembrances on the following pages covers a broad scope—from newborns to grandparents and delivery persons to friends far away—each of these diverse projects has one thing in common: it has been made as simple to complete as possible, including thorough, step-by-step instructions, with carefully thought-out diagrams and illustrations to help you duplicate the professional results shown.

We've even chosen gifts that are easy enough for kids to do—either by themselves or with a little assistance from Mom or Dad. Some will require adult supervision, but the actual crafting is geared to young fingers and quick results.

May the peace and joy of the Christmas season be yours as you craft gifts for those you love.

Chapter One

Gifts for Children & Teens

*F*rom the tiniest tot to the tallest teenager, children almost always top our Christmas gift lists.

Delight a new baby with colorful booties, a young boy with a play mat for his cars, or a special girl

with a topsy-turvy doll. Some of these gifts, like the duplicate-stitched sweater, can be completed

in a wink; others, like the planet mobile, take a bit longer. The techniques and skill levels vary,

but all of these gifts were created with very special young people in mind.

GOLDILOCKS AND THE THREE BEARS CARRY-ALONG HOUSE

$\mathcal{Y}$our favorite little girl will be able to take along the whole cast of characters, the furniture, and even the porridge! And it's all packed up in a magical traveling cottage. Sheets of plastic canvas inside the lightly padded walls and roof define the shape of the house and the sweet, stitched details make it like home.

⸺ ★ ⸺

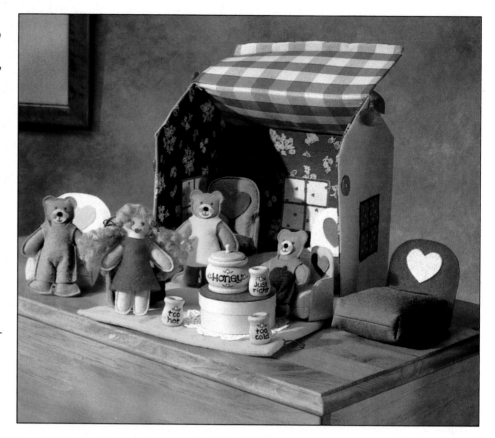

Sizes: 8¼ × 10½ × 10½-inch house; 4½- to 5-inch figures

MATERIALS

- ❊ Pencil
- ❊ Tracing paper
- ❊ Scissors
- ❊ Fabrics: 1 yard of yellow solid, ½ yard of blue print, ⅓ yard of red check, 12-inch square each of red print and white print
- ❊ 1 yard of fusible fleece
- ❊ Iron
- ❊ Two 12-inch squares of paper-backed fusible web
- ❊ Matching sewing thread
- ❊ Sewing machine
- ❊ Eight 10¾ × 13¾-inch sheets of plastic canvas
- ❊ Ribbons: 20-inch length of 1½-inch-wide red grosgrain; 48-inch length of ⅛-inch-wide red satin
- ❊ Two 1-inch red buttons

- ❊ 9 × 12-inch squares of felt: 3 pieces of turquoise; 2 pieces each of tan, red, green, and yellow; 1 piece each of peach, pink, white, and black
- ❊ 8 ounces of polyester fiberfill
- ❊ Paper punch
- ❊ Thick white craft glue
- ❊ Black, fine-point, permanent marker
- ❊ Ruler
- ❊ Blond curly wool doll hair
- ❊ Large-eyed needle
- ❊ 3½-inch-diameter wooden box with lid
- ❊ 5-inch-diameter white doily
- ❊ Small, pointed artist's brush
- ❊ Acrylic paints: black, red, yellow, and green
- ❊ 3 wooden candle cups
- ❊ 2-inch-high wooden pot with lid

DIRECTIONS

PREPARING THE PATTERNS

Enlarge the pattern pieces on page 19 as indicated. Trace the pattern pieces on pages 15 through 18 onto the tracing paper. Each pattern includes a ¼-inch seam allowance where needed. Cut out the pattern pieces.

MAKING THE HOUSE

$\mathcal{1}$ From the yellow fabric, cut five straight walls (two will be used for the floor) and two side walls. From the blue fabric, cut one

straight wall and two side walls. From the fusible fleece, cut three straight walls and two side walls.

2 Following the manufacturer's directions, fuse the paper-backed web to the wrong sides of the 12-inch squares of fabric. Mark one door and five windows on the paper side of the red print piece. Mark three windows and one heart for the door on the paper side of the white print piece. Cut out the shapes and peel away the paper.

3 Fuse the wrong side of one red print window to the right side of each of the yellow side walls, two red print windows to one yellow straight wall, and one red print window to one yellow straight wall, leaving space for the door on this wall. Place the door on this last yellow wall, then place the heart in position on the door. Fuse these two pieces to the wall. Fuse a white print window to each of the two side and one straight blue walls. Referring to the photograph, use blue or red thread and a medium-width zigzag stitch to machine appliqué along the edges of the windows, door, and heart. Appliqué straight lines across the center of the windows in each direction for the windowpane details.

4 Following the manufacturer's directions, fuse a piece of the fusible fleece to the wrong side of each of the four yellow walls with window and door appliqués, and to one of the yellow floor pieces.

5 With the right sides together, sew the plain yellow floor piece and the fleece-backed yellow floor piece together along the outer edges, leaving one short edge open. Turn right side out. Press, turning in ¼ inch along the open edges. Cut

one piece of plastic canvas ¼ inch smaller all around than the floor size. Slide the canvas into the floor section and topstitch the opening closed, as shown in **Diagram 1.**

Diagram 1

6 Construct each of the walls in the same way as the floor. Sew the wall with the door and a yellow wall together. Sew each of the yellow side walls to a blue side wall. Sew the remaining yellow and blue windowed wall pieces together.

7 From the red check, cut two roof pieces. Fuse fleece to the wrong side of one piece. With right sides together, sew the pieces together along three edges. Turn right side out, turn under ¼ inch along the open edges and press. Topstitch ¾ inch from the short edge opposite the opening, as shown in **Diagram 2.**

Diagram 2

8 Cut a 5 × 10-inch piece of plastic canvas. Insert this piece into the roof and against the top-stitching. Topstitch across the center of the roof, encasing the canvas piece, as shown in **Diagram 3.** Cut a second 5 × 10-inch piece of plastic canvas and insert this into the roof. Topstitch ¾ inch from the open

edge of the roof, encasing the second piece of canvas. Topstitch the opening closed.

Diagram 3

9 Sew the walls to the floor, stitching close to the edge of the pieces. Sew the side walls to the back wall. Leave the front wall free on the sides. Slip stitch the roof in place, sewing only the back half of the roof to the back peak of the side walls; leave the ¾-inch "eave" at the back free.

10 Knot the grosgrain ribbon 1 inch from each end. Sew each knot to the outside of the house at the roof peak for a handle. Sew a button to each front edge of a side wall, 1½ inches from the corner (see the photograph on page 12). Sew the center of a 12-inch length of the satin ribbon to one side of the front wall to match the button. Knot the ends of the ribbon together to create a loop that fits over the button. Repeat on the other side of the front wall. (*Optional*: Make the button loops with narrow elastic cord instead. The stretch makes fitting the loop over the button easier.)

MAKING THE FIGURES

1 Using the tan felt for the bears' bodies and the peach felt for Goldilocks' body, cut two rectangles of felt slightly larger than the patterns. Mark the body on one piece of felt. Place the two felt pieces together and sew about ⅛ inch inside the marked outline, leaving an opening for stuffing where marked. Cut the figure out of the felt, being sure to cut away all marked lines. Stuff each figure lightly, then sew the opening closed.

2 Cut a peach muzzle for each of the bears. Use the paper punch to cut two pink cheeks and one black nose for each bear from the felt. Use the craft glue to glue the nose and cheeks to the muzzle, then glue the muzzle in place. Use the marker to draw the mouth onto the muzzle and two eyes on the face above the muzzle, as shown in the photograph on page 12.

3 Use the paper punch to cut one red mouth, two pink cheeks, and two turquoise eyes from the felt. Glue these in place on Goldilocks' face. Use the marker to draw eyelashes and the sides of the smile. Cut two stretched 12-inch lengths of doll hair. Slightly part the center of each length and glue them to the top and back of the head. Fluff the ends of the hair. Thread a 7-inch length of the ⅛-inch-wide ribbon through the large-eyed needle and sew it through the side of the head. Tie the ends of the ribbon around the hair and into a bow. Repeat for the other side of the head.

4 Cut one apron from the yellow felt for the mama bear, then one apron from the red felt for

Goldilocks. Place an apron on each figure, overlapping and gluing the edges together in the back. Cut two overalls from the green felt for the papa bear and two overalls from the turquoise felt for the baby bear. Trim the back overall pieces where marked. Topstitch the front and back overall pieces together about ⅛ inch along each leg edge. Place the overalls on the figures, overlapping and gluing the straps together in the back.

MAKING THE TABLE AND DISHES

1 Cut a circle of red felt to fit the top of the round box lid, then glue the felt to the lid top. Glue the doily to the box bottom for a rug.

2 Referring to the photograph on page 12, paint the wooden candle cups with a phrase and a flower. Use black to paint "TOO HOT" on the first, "JUST RIGHT" on the second, and "TOO COLD" on the third. Paint four flowers and "HONEY" on the side of the wooden pot.

MAKING THE BEDS

1 Cut two 5⅛ × 6⅞-inch pieces each of red, turquoise, and pink felt for the mattresses. Using a ¼-inch seam allowance, sew the pairs of mattress pieces together along the outer edges, leaving an opening at the center of one short edge for turning.

2 Refold a corner so the seams meet. Sew across the corner about ½ inch from the point to miter the corner, as shown in **Diagram 4.** Repeat on the three remaining corners. Turn right side out. Stuff and slip stitch the opening closed.

Diagram 4

3 Using the white felt for two headboards and the red felt for one headboard, cut two rectangles of felt slightly larger than the pattern for each headboard. Mark the headboard on one felt rectangle. Place the two felt pieces together and sew about ⅛ inch inside the marked outline, leaving the bottom edge open. Cut the headboard out of the felt. Cut a piece of plastic canvas about ¼ inch smaller all around than the pattern for each headboard. Insert the canvas into the headboard and topstitch the opening closed. Cut and glue a heart of a contrasting color to each mattress and each headboard. Glue the white headboards to the pink and red mattresses, and the red headboard to the turquoise mattress.

MAKING THE CHAIRS

1 Using the green felt for the large chair, the turquoise felt for the medium chair, and the yellow felt for the small chair, cut two pieces of felt for each chair, slightly larger than the pattern. Mark the pattern on one piece of felt. Then sew the two felt pieces together inside the marked outline, leaving the bottom edge open. Topstitch a straight line from the corner of each arm to the bottom edge, as marked on the pattern by the dashed lines.

2 Cut a piece of plastic canvas to fit inside each of the three sections of the chair. Insert the plastic canvas piece into each chair section, then topstitch the bottom edge closed, as shown in **Diagram 5.**

Diagram 5

3 Cut two squares of felt in the same color as the chair for each chair seat: 3-inch squares for the small chair, 4-inch squares for the medium chair, and 4¾-inch squares for the large chair. Using a ¼-inch seam allowance, sew the two pieces together along the outer edges, leaving an opening at the center of one short edge. Use the same method as for the mattress to miter the corners, sewing across each corner ½ inch from the point for the small seat, ¾ inch from the point for the medium seat, and 1 inch from the point for the large seat. Turn right side out and stuff. Sew the opening closed.

4 Cut and glue a large heart of a contrasting color to the inside top of the medium and large chairs. Cut and glue a small heart of a contrasting color to the inside top of the small chair. Glue the chair to the seat, gluing the arms to the sides of the seat.

Baby Bear

Leave open

Cut here for back

Baby's Overalls

**Papa
and
Mama Bear**

Leave open

Cut here for back

**Papa's
Overalls**

Apron

Goldilocks

Leave open

Headboard

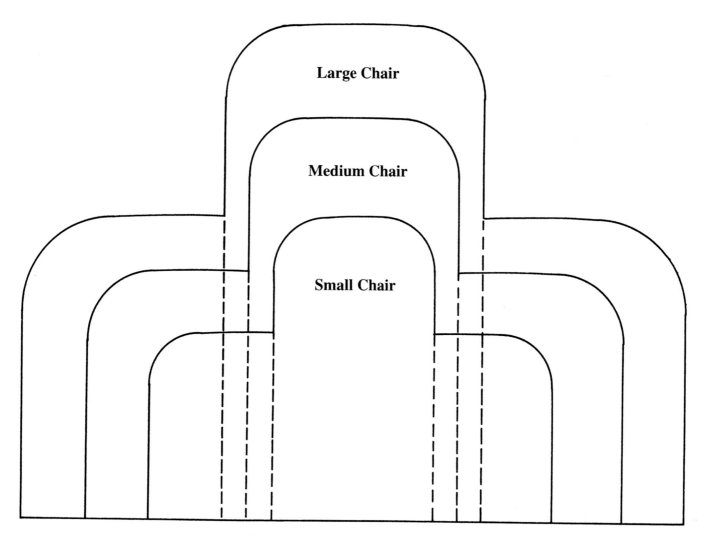

Large Chair

Medium Chair

Small Chair

Large Heart

Door

Window

Small Heart

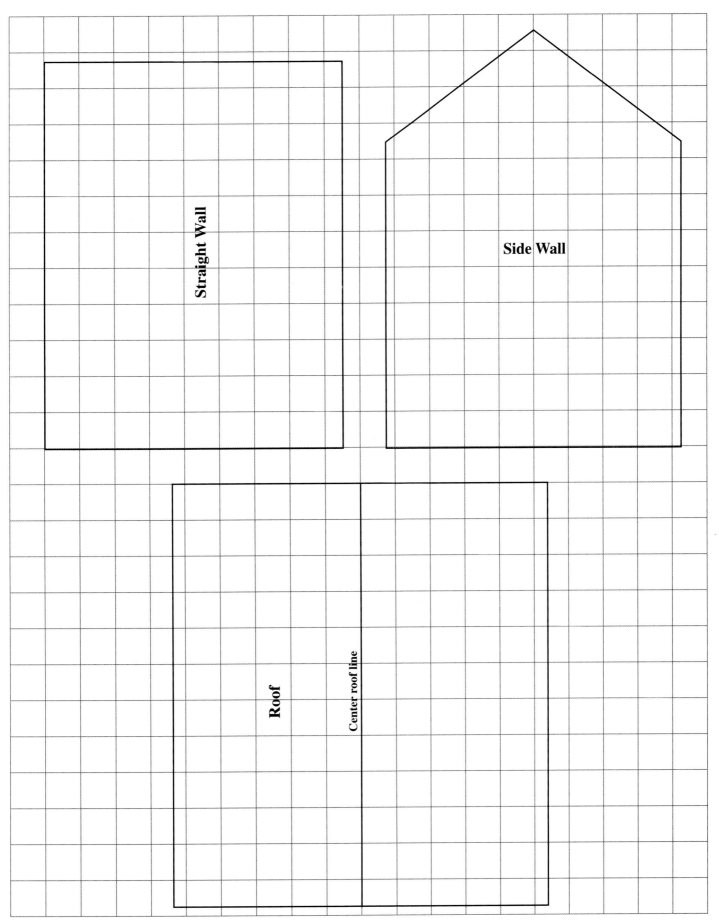

Straight Wall

Side Wall

Roof

Center roof line

1 square = 1 inch

Enlarge 267%

PLANET AND STARS MOBILE

A budding astronaut will dream of other worlds with this mobile as inspiration. A combination of soft sculpture and glow-in-the-dark clay stars creates a colorful galaxy. Bright prints and metallic fabric scraps re-create a space shuttle and satellite as well as a variety of planets. Your young scientist will experience the thrill of space travel with this dramatic accent.

Size: 17 inches from tip to tip of crossbars

MATERIALS

✳ Sandpaper
✳ Inner ring of a 12-inch wooden embroidery hoop
✳ Water-soluble marking pen
✳ Thick white craft glue
✳ Two ⅛-inch-diameter wooden dowels, each 17 inches long
✳ Paintbrush
✳ White acrylic paint, or paint color to blend with ceiling color
✳ Paint sealer
✳ Lightweight iron-on interfacing to stabilize woven lamé fabrics
✳ Assorted lamé scraps, including silver, textured gold, copper, and gold
✳ Pencil
✳ Tracing paper
✳ Scissors

✳ Assorted calico fabrics, including 4 blues, 1 purple, 1 red, and 1 brown
✳ Sewing machine
✳ Matching sewing thread, including metallic thread
✳ Polyester fiberfill
✳ Hand-sewing needle
✳ Toothpicks
✳ Black fabric paint
✳ Compass
✳ Ruler
✳ Pins
✳ 18-gauge floral wire
✳ Polymer clay, such as Fimo Night Glow*
✳ Monofilament thread
✳ Large-eyed, sharp needle
See the "Buyer's Guide" on page 176.

DIRECTIONS

PREPARING THE WOODEN PIECES

1 Sand the surface of the embroidery hoop smooth, if necessary, to remove any splinters. Referring to **Diagram 1** and using the marking pen, mark the outer edge of the hoop in quarters, placing two marks opposite each other on the top edge of the hoop, and the other two marks opposite each other on the bottom edge of the hoop. These marks will position one length of the wooden dowel across the top of the hoop and the other length of the wooden dowel as a crossbar across the bottom of the hoop.

Diagram 1

2 Use the sandpaper to sand a notch into the hoop edge at each mark. Make the notches deep enough to hold the ⅛-inch dowels securely.

3 Glue the dowels into the sanded notches, as shown in **Diagram 2,** centering the dowels across the hoop. Add a dot of glue to the dowels where they cross.

Diagram 2

4 Apply a coat of white paint (or ceiling color) to the hoop and wooden dowels. Let the paint dry thoroughly. Paint a second coat if necessary. Apply a coat of paint sealer to these wooden pieces and let them dry thoroughly.

PREPARING THE FABRIC

Woven lamé fabrics fray easily and should be stabilized with fusible interfacing to make the fabric easier to work with. Following the manufacturer's directions, use a low steam setting to fuse the lightweight interfacing to the wrong side of the woven lamé pieces before cutting the pattern shapes.

MAKING THE PLANETS

1 Trace the planet segment patterns on pages 23 and 24 onto the tracing paper. Trace the planet ring patterns onto paper. Add ¼-inch seam allowances to all the pattern edges before cutting out each pattern piece.

2 Use the patterns to cut four pieces from the same calico fabric for each planet, making one A planet in red, one B planet in purple, one C planet each in blue and brown, and one D planet in blue. With right sides facing, sew the four segments of each planet together, leaving about a 1½-inch opening on one seam for turning, as shown in **Diagram 3.** Clip the seams and turn right side out. Stuff the planet firmly and slip stitch the opening closed.

Diagram 3

3 For each of the C and D planet rings, cut two pieces each from the remaining two blue fabrics. Sew a line of stay stitching along the inner edge of each ring piece. With right sides facing, sew the matching ring pieces together along the outer edge. Clip the outer seam edges and turn right side out. Stuff the rings very lightly. Turn under the seam allowance along the inner edge of each ring piece, and sew the inner edges together. Place the rings on the corresponding planet at the desired angle, and tack in place, sewing the tacking stitches on opposite sides of the planet.

MAKING THE SPACE SHUTTLE

1 Trace the space shuttle pattern pieces on page 23 onto paper, adding ³⁄₁₆-inch seam allowances to all edges. From the silver lamé, cut the space shuttle body, base, and tail.

2 With right sides facing, sew the nose seam of the body. With right sides facing, sew the body and base together, sewing from marked point A around the shuttle wing, nose, and other wing to marked point B, as shown in **Diagram 4.** (The shorter space between A and B remains open for turning.) Clip the curves and turn right side out.

Diagram 4

3 Stuff the wings very lightly. Sew a line of top stitching through both fabric layers and along the inner edge of each wing to the nose, as marked on the **Space Shuttle Body** pattern by the dashed lines. Firmly stuff the remaining body of the shuttle. Fold down the rear flap of the body piece, turn under the seam allowance, and slip stitch the flap in place to close the shuttle body, as shown in **Diagram 5.**

Diagram 5

4 With right sides facing, sew the two tail pieces together, leaving the bottom edge open. Clip the curves and turn right side out. Turn under the remaining seam allowance at the bottom and slip stitch the tail in position on the back of the shuttle, as shown in the photograph on page 20.

5 Use toothpicks to apply black paint "windows" to the front of the shuttle; refer to the photograph for placement.

MAKING THE SATELLITE

1 Use the compass to draw a 2⅜-inch circle on the tracing paper for the base cylinder pattern and a 1⅛-inch circle for the upper cylinder pattern.

2 For the satellite base, cut two 2⅜-inch circles and one 1½ × 4¾-inch rectangle from the textured gold lamé. For the upper cylinder, cut one 1⅛-inch circle and one ⅞ × 3-inch rectangle from the copper lamé. Also cut three gold and one copper lamé pieces, each 1¼ × 5 inches, for the solar panels. Each fabric piece includes a ³⁄₁₆-inch seam allowance.

3 With right sides facing, fold each solar panel piece in half crosswise. Sew each long edge of each panel, leaving the short edge opposite the fold open for turning. Turn each panel right side out and turn under the seam allowance at the open edge. Pin in place.

4 To topstitch the grid pattern on each panel, begin by sewing two lines lengthwise on the panel, dividing the piece into thirds. Sew cross lines every ¼ inch along the length of the panel to complete the grid.

5 Cut two 5-inch lengths of wire. Slide a panel onto each end of each wire length, slipping the wire between and through the topstitching all the way to the end of the panel and having the open ends of the panels facing each other at the center of the wire, as shown in **Diagram 6.**

Diagram 6

6 Place the panel pairs together, crossing them at the center. Wrap thread around the crossed wires to secure the panels, as shown in **Diagram 7.** Cut a ½-inch square of gold lamé and glue it in place to cover the crossed wires or, if desired, wrap metallic thread around each exposed wire to cover it.

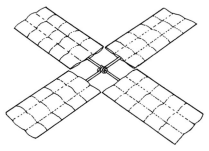

Diagram 7

7 With right sides facing, fold the satellite base rectangle in half and sew the narrow ends of the rectangle together to form a tube, leaving a small opening for turning. Sew a 2⅜-inch fabric circle to each end of the tube. Clip the curves and turn the satellite base right side out. Stuff the base and sew the opening closed.

8 Fold in half and sew the narrow ends of the upper cylinder together to form a tube. Hand sew the 1⅛-inch fabric circle to one end of the tube. Clip the curves and turn right side out. Lightly stuff the upper cylinder, turn under the seam allowances at the open edge, and slip stitch the cylinder in the center of one end of the base cylinder, as shown in **Diagram 8.** Center the crossed solar panels on top of the upper cylinder and tack in place, adding a dab of glue to hold them securely.

Diagram 8

9 To make the stars, begin by kneading the clay until it is malleable. Roll out the clay to about ⅛ inch thick. Draw eight free-hand stars of different sizes on paper. Cut these out and use them for star patterns. Place the patterns on the clay and use a pin or toothpick to mark the inner and outer points of each star. Use a knife or scissors to cut out each star shape from the clay. Poke a hanging hole in the top point of each star. Bake the clay stars, following the manufacturer's directions.

ASSEMBLING THE MOBILE

1 Cut two 28-inch lengths of monofilament. Tie each monofilament end to opposite ends of a dowel at the hoop edge, adjusting the ties so that the hoop is balanced

when the monofilaments are held in the center, as shown in **Diagram 9.** Use another piece of monofilament to tie a hanging loop at the center of the dowel filaments.

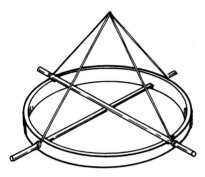

Diagram 9

2 Thread monofilament through a large-eyed needle and sew a generous length of monofilament to the top of each planet, the shuttle, and the satellite. Tie a length of monofilament through the hole in each star. Use a double knot to secure each monofilament, adding a dab of glue to seal each knot.

3 Tie the fabric shapes to the hoop and dowels, as shown in the photograph on page 20, or as desired. Vary the lengths at which the shapes hang, taking care to keep the mobile balanced. Attach the stars last.

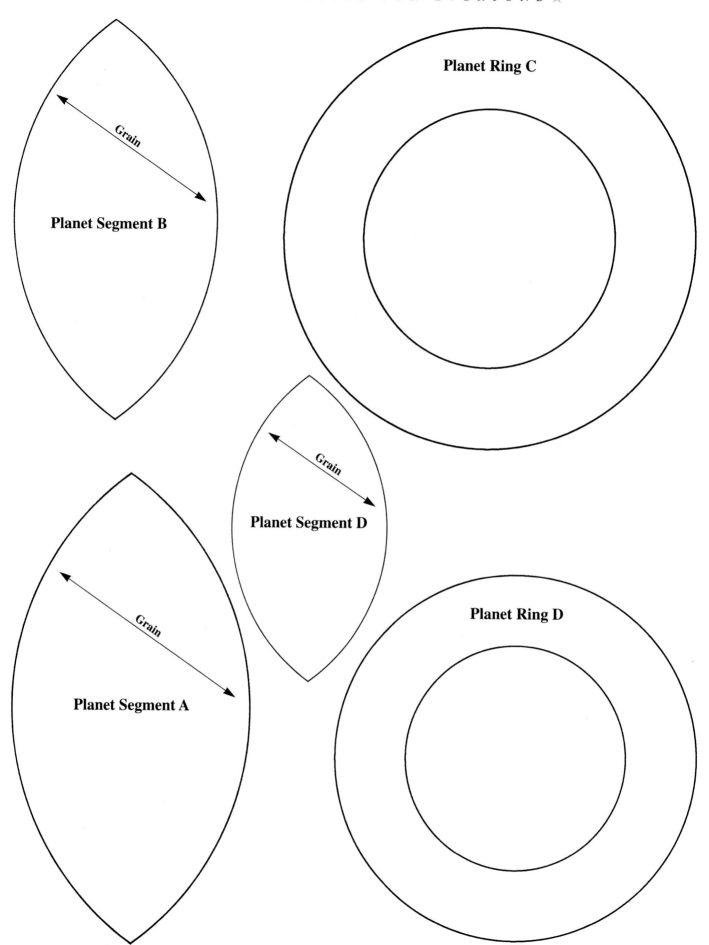

LITTLE RED RIDING HOOD TOPSY-TURVY DOLL

Telling this favorite old tale will be brand-new fun for a child, when you illustrate it with all three of the story's characters. Little Red Riding Hood highlights this whimsical topsy-turvy design. A quick flip of the calico skirt will reveal either Granny or the Big Bad Wolf, depending on the placement of the nightcap.

Size: About 14 inches tall

DIRECTIONS

1 Trace the pattern pieces on pages 28 through 30, including markings, onto the tracing paper. Each pattern includes a ¼-inch seam allowance, except where noted. Cut out the pattern pieces.

2 From the peach fabric, cut three heads and six hands. From the gray fabric, cut one head and two hands. From the red print and blue check, cut two bodies each. From the gray felt, cut one nose and two ears. Transfer pattern markings to the fabrics with the marking pen.

3 With right sides facing, pin and sew a peach head to the neck of each red body piece, and sew a peach hand at each wrist. Sew a peach head and hands to one blue-check body piece in the same way. Sew the gray head and gray hands to the second blue-check body piece. Press all the seams open. Baste the ears to the gray head between the ear placement marks, folding each ear at the front edge, as shown in **Diagram 1.**

Diagram 1

4 With the right sides facing, sew the red body pieces together, leaving the waist edge open. Sew the blue-check body pieces together in the same way. Clip the seams at the neck and underarm corners. Turn one of the bodies right side out. Tuck this body inside the other so that the right sides of the fabrics are facing and the seams match. Sew the waist edges together, as shown in **Diagram 2,** leaving an opening for turning. Turn right side out. Firmly stuff both bodies with the polyester fiberfill, and slip stitch the opening closed.

Diagram 2

5 Fold the nose in half along the straight edge. Using a ¼-inch seam allowance, sew along the straight edge. Turn right side out and stuff with fiberfill. Use matching thread to sew the nose in place on the gray head, then sew the pink pom-pom to the tip of the nose.

6 Cut a ⅜ × 2¾-inch piece of white felt, pinking one long edge of the strip for the wolf's teeth. Referring to **Diagram 3,** sew the strip to the base of the nose in a U shape. Cut a red felt tongue and tack it to the nose at the curved end of the teeth.

Diagram 3

7 Use a pencil to lightly mark two ⅛-inch-diameter circles on the gray head for the wolf's eyes (see the photograph on page 25 for placement). Use three strands of the black embroidery floss to satin stitch the eyes.

8 On the opposite side of the wolf's head, lightly mark the outlines for granny's mouth, nose, ¼-inch-diameter eyes, and eyeglasses, as shown in the photograph on page 25. Using three strands of brown embroidery floss, satin stitch the eyes. Using three strands of floss, backstitch the nose with brown, the mouth with red, and the eyeglasses with blue. Use the pink crayon or cosmetic blush to color the cheeks.

9 Hand sew a length of eyelet along the seam edge of the gray/peach head. Then hand sew a second piece of eyelet around the entire neck.

FOLDING PLAY MAT

You could call it Christmas Town or Our Town, but either way some lucky young city planner is going to have hours of fun "driving" through this village. And what town would be complete without a three-dimensional parking garage for small cars and trucks? The whole town folds flat for quick cleanup or easy travel. It's sure to be a hit whether you follow our directions for lettering the buildings or label them to match those on the child's hometown Main Street.

Size: 28 × 34 inches when flat

MATERIALS

❋ 8 × 14½-inch piece of turquoise cotton fabric
❋ Sewing machine
❋ Matching sewing thread
❋ Water-soluble marking pen
❋ Thin cardboard
❋ Iron
❋ Scissors
❋ 1¼ yards of unbleached canvas, 60 inches wide
❋ Masking tape
❋ Pencil
❋ Ruler
❋ Flat artist's brush
❋ Fabric paints in assorted colors
❋ Black and gray fine-point fabric markers

DIRECTIONS

MAKING THE GARAGE

1 Fold under ¼ inch along the long edges of the 8 × 14½-inch turquoise piece. Topstitch close to the folded edges.

2 On the right side of the fabric, use the marking pen to mark the placement of two center stitching lines along the lengthwise center of the piece, ½ inch apart, as shown in **Diagram 1.** These will be the lines for stitching the garage to the mat.

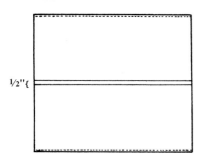

Diagram 1

3 Referring to **Diagram 2,** mark the wrong side of the fabric with lines to divide the piece into segments.

Diagram 2

4 Using the thin cardboard as a straight edge, press sharp creases in the fabric along these lines, as shown in **Diagram 3.** The 2-inch segments form the garage roofs and the ⅜-inch segments form the accordion-style pleats for the garage sides. Baste the pleats in place inside the two marked center stitching lines. Press under ¼ inch on the two short edges of the garage.

Diagram 3

5 Cut a 30 × 36-inch piece of canvas. Fold it in half lengthwise to mark the center.

6 Referring to **Diagram 4,** place the center of the garage on the center of the canvas 1 inch from the left edge.

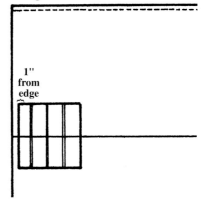

Diagram 4

7 Topstitch the side edges of the garage in place, leaving the roof edges of the end garages free, as shown in **Diagram 5.** Topstitch along each of the parking space stitching lines, then along each of the center stitching lines. Remove basting stitches.

Diagram 5

MAKING THE MAT

1 Use the masking tape to mark the roadway edges on the canvas with the garage, beginning 1 inch in on all sides and referring to the **Road Diagram** on page 34 for measurements. Press the tape securely to the fabric.

2 Referring to the **Building Diagram** on page 35, mark the buildings, doors, windows, and signs on the streets, using a pencil and a ruler for straight lines.

3 Paint the grass and buildings in colors as shown in the photograph on page 31, or as desired. Let each paint color dry thoroughly before proceeding to the next color. Next, paint the building details such as windows and doors. Use the markers for outlines and other fine-lined details, such as the signs and the center lines in the roads.

FINISHING THE PLAY MAT

1 Trim the painted mat to 29 × 35 inches. Use this piece as a pattern to cut another piece of canvas for the back of the mat. With right sides facing, use a ½-inch seam allowance to sew these pieces together, leaving an 8-inch opening for turning. Trim the corners and turn the mat right side out. Turn in the seam allowances at the opening, then topstitch around the entire outer edge of the mat.

2 Cut two 4 × 22-inch pieces of canvas for the mat handles. Fold the long edges of each handle

piece to the center and press the folded edges, as shown in **Diagram 6,** fold each piece in half lengthwise, then topstitch each long edge on each handle.

Diagram 6

3 Fold under ⅝ inch at each end of each handle and press. Place the handle on the long edge of the unpainted side of the mat with the ends 3 inches apart and 5 inches in from the edge, as shown in **Diagram 7.** Sew these ends in place with a ⅝-inch square of stitching, as shown in the diagram.

Diagram 7

4 Fold the mat in thirds along the length, folding the garage in first. Fold the mat in half crosswise, bringing the handles together, as shown in **Diagram 8.**

Diagram 8

Road Diagram

1 square = 1 inch   **Enlarge 448%**

Building Diagram

POSY POWER SWEATER

*S*titch a blast from the past! It's "flower power" for today's teens. Just toss a bouquet of flowers onto

a sweater and duplicate stitch the designs in the colors of your choice. Combine solidly stitched flowers with outlined ones.

Or save time—and stitching—by working only outlined blossoms. If you want to create a sweater for a toddler,

embroider only the smaller motif and scatter it around the garment.

Size: As desired

MATERIALS

❋ Heavyweight cotton pullover
  in any solid color, with a gauge
  of about 5 stitches and 7 rows to
  1 inch
❋ Six-strand embroidery floss in
  desired colors: 1 skein for a
  large flower center, 3 skeins
  for a large solid flower, 1 skein
  for a large flower outline or for
  a small solid or outlined flower
❋ Size 22 tapestry needle

DIRECTIONS

1 Working with six strands of floss
in the needle, and following the
chart for small or large flowers,
duplicate stitch flowers randomly on
the sweater.

2 Begin each flower with a solid
center, then stitch the petal
outlines. Leave some of these petals
as outlines, but fill in others as
desired; refer to the photograph on
the opposite page for stitching ideas.

Duplicate Stitch

Duplicate stitch is an embroidery
stitch used to "duplicate" the
look of plain knit stitches. Quick
to learn and easy to do, duplicate stitch simply retraces the
path of the original knit stitch.
Keep your stitches even and take
care not to pull them too tightly.

HERE'S HOW:

Thread a blunt needle with
embroidery floss. Bring the needle up from the wrong side to the
right side of your garment in the
space below the stitch you wish to
duplicate. Thread it from front-to-
back-to-front around the top of
the stitch, then back down
through the original stitch space
to the wrong side. Adjust the floss
to cover the base stitch. Stitches
can be worked in either horizontal
or vertical rows. If the design
calls for you to skip over more
than three stitches, end your floss
length and begin again so you
won't carry the floss across the
wrong side of the garment.

Posy Power Sweater Chart

PANSIES AND ROSEBUDS
RIBBON JEWELRY

Ladies will be delighted to receive these charming posies. Create flower-covered clips to nip in the waistlines of jackets and vests. Add a matching pair of earrings to complete the picture. Wired French ribbons make the crafting of these lovely accessories a simple matter. Choose from any number of natural floral colors.

Sizes: 2¼ × 6½-inch jacket clips;
1 × 2½-inch earrings

BASIC FLOWER SHAPES

DIRECTIONS

1 To make the rosebud: Use one color of wire ribbon. Cut a length proportionate to the size of the flower you want to make and fold the ribbon in half lengthwise. Wrap one end of the ribbon around your forefinger to create a cone, as shown in **Diagram 1.**

Diagram 1

Twist the ribbon a half twist, and continue to loosely wrap the end around your finger, as shown in **Diagram 2.** Wrap the entire length of ribbon around the finger, twisting the ribbon once or twice each wrap. Slip the rosebud from your finger and tuck the end of the ribbon into the bottom of the center cone to finish the bud. Slip stitch the ribbon end in place.

Diagram 2

2 To make the pansy: Use two different colors of wire ribbon, one darker than the other. Cut a 6-inch length of the darker color ribbon and a 7½-inch length of the lighter color ribbon. Mark the center of the 6-inch ribbon; mark the 7½-inch ribbon every 2½ inches. Use matching sewing thread to hand sew semicircular lines of gathering stitches along the length of the ribbon between the marks, as shown in **Diagram 3.**

Diagram 3

Gently pull the thread to gather the ribbon into petal shapes. The gathers will be at the bottom of the petals, as shown in **Diagram 4.**

Diagram 4

Sew the two-petal piece to the bottom of the three-petal piece to form the pansy, as shown in **Diagram 5.** Glue a bead, if needed, in the center of the three-petal piece to create a flower center.

Diagram 5

3 To make the folded leaf: Cut a 3-inch length of green ribbon. Using the marking pen, mark the middle of the piece. Fold each end of the piece over to meet the center mark of the ribbon, as shown in **Diagram 6.**

Diagram 6

Make a small pleat on each side of the folded leaf, as shown in **Diagram 7,** and tack it in place at the bottom with two or three stitches. Attach the leaf to a flower or other leaves.

Diagram 7

PANSIES JACKET CLIP

MATERIALS

❊ 1½-inch-wide wire-edged taffeta ribbons, such as from Offray ribbon: 18-inch length of green, 10-inch length of pink, 7½-inch length of yellow, and 6-inch length of purple*
❊ 6 × 8mm oval yellow bead
❊ 8-inch length of ⅞-inch-wide green wire-edged taffeta ribbon
❊ 10-inch length of 1½-inch-wide dark green grosgrain ribbon
❊ Pair of suspender clips
*See the "Buyer's Guide" on page 176.

DIRECTIONS

1 Referring to the "Basic Flower Shape" directions on page 39, use the purple and yellow ribbons to make a pansy. Glue the bead in the center of the flower. Use 5-inch lengths of pink ribbon to make two rosebuds. Use 3-inch lengths of the 1½-inch-wide green taffeta ribbon to make six folded leaves, and 2-inch lengths of the ⅞-inch-wide green ribbon to make four smaller folded leaves.

2 Thread each end of the 10-inch lengths of grosgrain ribbon through a suspender clip. Overlap the ribbon ends in the center of the loop that is formed. Fold under ¼ inch on the overlapped ribbon and slip stitch the ends in place, as shown in the **Clip Diagram.**

Clip Diagram

3 Use the glue gun to glue the flowers and leaves to the ribbon loop. Refer to the photograph on page 38 for placement. Begin with the end leaves and work toward the center. Glue the pansy on last.

ROSEBUD JACKET CLIP

MATERIALS

❊ 1½-inch-wide wire-edged taffeta ribbons, such as from Offray ribbon: 18-inch length of orange, 16-inch length of pink*
❊ 22-inch length of ⅞-inch-wide green wire-edged taffeta ribbon
❊ 10-inch length of 1½-inch-wide dark green grosgrain ribbon
❊ Pair of suspender clips
❊ 16-inch length of ⅜-inch-wide gold chiffon wire-edged ribbon
❊ 1-inch-tall cupid charm
*See the "Buyer's Guide" on page 176.

DIRECTIONS

1 Referring to the "Basic Flower Shape" directions on page 39, use 8-inch lengths of pink ribbon for two rosebuds. Use an 8-inch length of orange for one rosebud and two 5-inch lengths for two smaller rosebuds. Use 2-inch lengths of the ⅞-inch-wide green taffeta ribbon for 11 folded leaves.

2 Thread each end of the 10-inch length of grosgrain through a suspender clip. Overlap the ends in the center of the loop that is formed. Fold under ¼ inch on the overlapped ribbon and slip stitch the ends in place. Refer to the **Clip Diagram.**

3 Use the glue gun to glue the flowers and leaves to the gros-

grain ribbon loop, referring to the **Placement Diagram.** Begin with the end leaves first, working toward the center. Glue the rosebuds on next. Tie the gold chiffon ribbon into a bow and glue it below the center rosebud. Hand tack the charm below the center of the bow.

Placement Diagram

ROSEBUD EARRINGS

MATERIALS

❊ ⅞-inch-wide wire-edged taffeta ribbons, such as from Offray ribbon: 12-inch length of green, 10-inch length each of orange and pink*
❊ Pair of ¾-inch-diameter earring backs
❊ Two 1-inch-tall cupid charms
*See the "Buyer's Guide" on page 176.

DIRECTIONS

1 Referring to the "Basic Flower Shape" directions on page 39, use 5-inch lengths of ribbon for two rosebuds, one in pink and one in orange. Use 2-inch lengths of the green ribbon for six folded leaves.

2 Use the glue gun to glue the flowers and leaves to the earring back, referring to the photograph on page 38 for placement. Glue the three leaves first and the orange and pink rosebuds next. Hand tack the charm below the lower rosebud. Repeat for the other earring, facing the leaves in the opposite direction.

VIDEO GAME RACK

$\mathcal{A}$ gift that doubles as storage is certainly always welcome in a teenager's room. Craft a rack to keep video games lined up and identifiable at a glance. Wooden dowels separate each game, making retrieval a snap. By varying the distance between the dowels, you can use the same system to organize videos or tapes. By increasing the length of the base, you can organize even more games! As an added treat, stick a new video in with the gift.

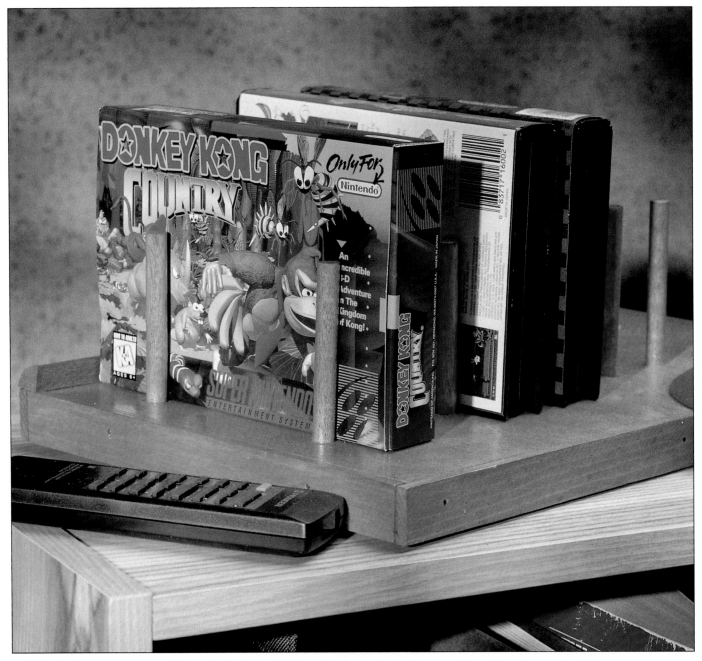

Size: 8½ × 15 inches

MATERIALS

* Ruler
* Hand saw
* 4 feet of 1-inch-wide wooden furring strip
* 6 feet of ⅜-inch wood doweling
* 16-inch length of ½-inch quarter-round molding
* Sandpaper
* Pencil
* 8½ × 15-inch piece of ¾-inch clear interior-grade plywood
* Masking tape
* Electric drill with ⅜-inch wood drill bit
* Wood stain in desired color
* Paintbrush
* Carpenter's glue
* Brads
* Polyurethane varnish

DIRECTIONS

1 Cut the furring strip into four lengths: two 8½-inch lengths and two 15½-inch lengths.

2 Cut eighteen 4-inch lengths from the ⅜-inch wood doweling. These will be used for the pegs.

3 Trim the quarter-round molding to 15½ inches.

4 Sand the cut edges of all the wood pieces smooth.

5 Use the pencil to mark the peg positions on the plywood piece. Mark two rows of nine holes each along the 15-inch length of the plywood. Referring to the **Video Game Rack Diagram,** place the first row 2 inches from the top edge and the second row 3 inches from the lower edge, with the first

holes 1 inch from the left and right edges, and adjacent holes 1⅝ inches apart. Drill a ½-inch-deep hole at each peg marking.

6 Using the paintbrush, stain each wood piece. Let the stain dry thoroughly.

7 Using the carpenter's glue, glue a peg into each hole in the plywood piece.

8 Glue and nail the furring strip pieces in place on the short ends of the plywood. Then glue and nail the long furring strip pieces to the long edges of the plywood. Glue and nail the quarter-round molding in place along the back edge.

9 Varnish the surfaces of the game rack, including the pegs. Let the varnish dry thoroughly.

Better Woodworking Results

❄

When using both stain and glue in a woodworking project, always stain each component before gluing. Glue fills the pores of the wood, creating a smooth surface that will not accept stain.

❄

When drilling a number of ½-inch holes, make sure each hole is the same depth by wrapping a piece of masking tape around the drill bit ½ inch from the end. Stop drilling when the masking tape reaches the plywood.

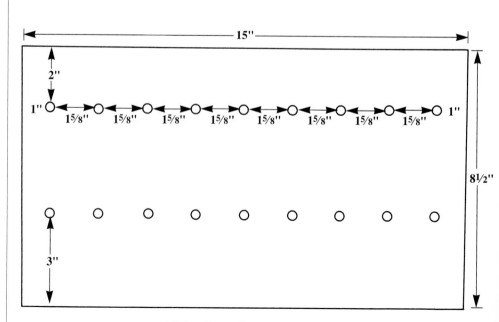

Video Game Rack Diagram

SWITCHEMS GAME

*W*hat a smart Santa to leave this brand new game! More challenging than tic-tac-toe and quicker to learn and play than checkers, it's fun for players of all ages. It's small enough to take along on trips and brightly colored enough not to get lost among other travel possessions. It's a snap to make from small squares of synthetic suede; use felt for a less-expensive version, if you prefer.

Size: About 9 × 13 inches unrolled

MATERIALS

❋ 9 × 12-inch pieces of Ultrasuede synthetic suede: 2 of orange and 1 each of turquoise and chartreuse (*Nancy's Notions* has 9 × 12-inch pieces of Ultrasuede available by mail order.)*

❋ Scissors or craft knife

❋ Ruler and pencil

❋ Masking tape

❋ 2 contrasting shades of fabric paint, such as Duncan Scribbles fashion paint in white and red*

❋ Paintbrush

❋ Fabric glue

❋ Sewing machine and thread to match the fabrics

❋ 1 yard of ⅜-inch-wide double-faced satin or grosgrain ribbon

❋ 12 playing pieces such as bingo markers: 4 each of 2 colors

*See the "Buyer's Guide" on page 176.

DIRECTIONS

1 From the two orange fabric pieces, cut one 9-inch square and one 9 × 9¼-inch piece; the extra ¼ inch on the second piece is a seam allowance for attaching the pocket. Set the 9-inch square aside.

2 On the wrong side of the larger orange piece, with the ruler and pencil, mark a 1¼-inch border on three sides and a 1½-inch border on the fourth side (this includes the ¼-inch seam allowance), as shown in **Diagram 1** at right.

3 Mark the center area into a grid of sixteen 1⅝-inch squares, as shown in **Diagram 2** at right.

Diagram 1

Diagram 2

4 Place the masking tape along the outside edges of alternate squares to keep the lines straight

43

The Game of Switchems

OBJECT:
The object of the game is to be the first to switch your pieces with the pieces of your opponent.

SETUP:
Arrange the two four-token teams in two opposite corners, as shown in the diagram at right.

RULES:
1. The younger player starts the first game. After that the winner goes first.

2. You may jump out from your home corner over your own piece.
3. Once a piece leaves its home corner, it may not return.
4. You must leave your home corner if your opponent is ready to enter it and has no other useful move.

PLAY:
1. A piece may move into any adjacent vacant square, including diagonally.
2. Begin the game by moving any piece out of your home corner.

3. Alternate moves, following the rules, until the game's been won.

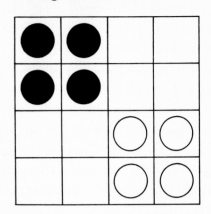

---

when painting. Paint squares with one paint color for the checkerboard pattern. Let the paint dry, then move the masking tape to paint the remaining squares with the other paint color.

5 Mark a 1¼-inch border on all the edges of the reserved 9-inch square and cut out the center area. Use the glue to affix this "frame" onto the larger, painted piece, making sure the frame edges meet or just cover the painted edges; remember to leave the ¼-inch seam allowance free. Use matching thread to machine topstitch the inner and outer edges of the frame, as shown in **Diagram 3.**

Diagram 3

6 From the turquoise fabric, cut a 5½ × 9-inch rectangle for the pocket back and flap. From the

chartreuse fabric, cut a 3⅜ × 9-inch rectangle for the pocket front. Referring to **Diagram 4,** place the pocket front and back together with the wrong sides facing and the one long and two short edges evenly aligned. Use the glue to hold the edges together, then machine topstitch along those three edges, leaving the top edge open.

Diagram 4

7 Mark a line on the pocket back ¼ inch above the top of the front. Lay the game board with the checkerboard side up, and run a bead of glue along the ¼-inch seam allowance. Position the pocket, with the pocket front up, on the seam allowance so that the marked line matches the seam line, as shown in **Diagram 5.** Fold out the pocket flap so the fold of the pocket is against the edge of the game board and topstitch close to the pocket opening, sewing through the three layers.

Diagram 5

8 From the turquoise fabric, cut four ½-inch squares. Glue one square to each corner of the game board. Referring to **Diagram 6,** tack the ribbon to the back of the game board (the outside of the roll) by placing the game board face side down and laying the ribbon along the center; securely tack the ribbon in place to the frame's inner stitching line opposite the pocket.

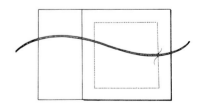

Diagram 6

9 Place the playing pieces in the pocket, roll up the board, and use the ribbon to tie the game closed.

RATTLE BABY BLOCKS

Filled with soft fiberfill, these blocks are easy for little fingers to grasp. When little hands hold and shake the blocks, the built-in rattle provides even more interest. Choose bright colors and simple shapes to appeal to baby. The small amounts of fabric required for the project make these blocks a perfect way to use up leftover scraps.

Size: Each block is 5 × 5 × 5 inches

MATERIALS

❋ Iron
❋ Six 4¾-inch squares of paper-backed fusible web for each block
❋ Six 5-inch squares of assorted print fabrics for each block
❋ Scissors and pinking shears
❋ Six 5½-inch squares of assorted print fabrics for each block
❋ Sewing machine (with decorative stitch optional)
❋ Matching sewing thread
❋ Polyester fiberfill
❋ Empty thread spool for each block
❋ 3-inch length of cardboard paper towel tube for each block

DIRECTIONS

1 Following the manufacturer's directions, use the iron to fuse a web square to the wrong side of each 5-inch square of print fabric.

2 From each fused 5-inch square, use your pinking shears to cut a 2¾-inch square or a heart or star pattern on page 46. Fuse the patterns to the center of each 5½-inch square of print fabric. If desired, embellish the shape by sewing a decorative machine stitch around the edges of the shapes.

3 Using a ¼-inch seam allowance and with right sides facing each other, sew four 5½-inch squares together to form a strip. Then, sew a 5½-inch square to the top and bottom edges of the second square of the strip, as shown in **Diagram 1.**

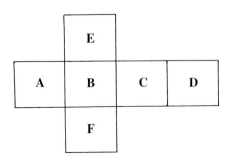

Diagram 1

4 Referring to the lettered blocks in **Diagram 1** on page 45 and having right sides facing, sew the top edge of A to the left edge of E, as shown in **Diagram 2.**

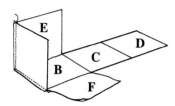

Diagram 2

5 Sew the right edge of E to the top edge of C and the bottom edge of C to the right edge of F, as shown in **Diagram 3.** Sew the left edge of F to the bottom edge of A. Sew around two of the three remaining open sides of D. Turn the block right side out.

Diagram 3

6 Stuff the block slightly with fiberfill. Insert the spool into the center of the cardboard tube. Insert a small amount of fiberfill at each end of the tube; leave enough room in the tube for the spool to move. Insert the tube into the block. Finish stuffing the block, being sure to surround the tube. Slip stitch the opening closed.

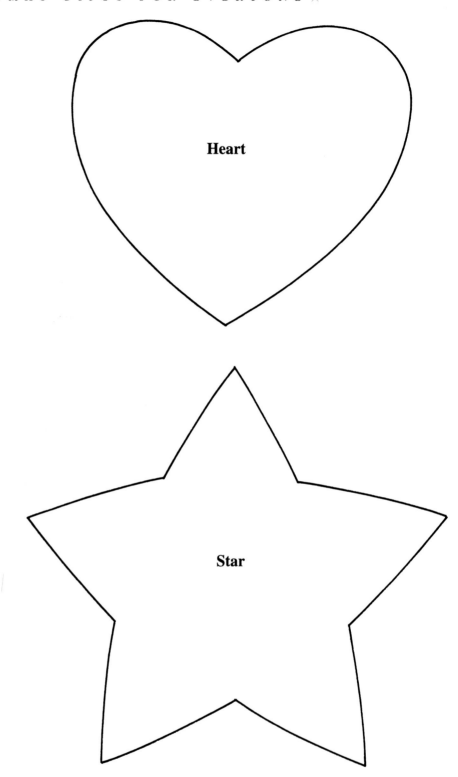

Heart

Star

FANCY FEET FELT BOOTIES

*W*hether a gift for a wee woodsman or a budding ballerina, choose the perfect felt footgear to get him or her

off and running. The Santa and elf booties will get everyone into the holiday act, while the

saddle shoe and cowboy booties lend a whimsical air to pint-sized baby togs.

Size: 12–18 months

DIRECTIONS

Trace the pattern pieces on pages 51 through 53 onto the tracing paper. Trace a full bootie pattern so it will be easier to fit the pattern on the felt pieces. Each pattern includes the ¼-inch seam allowance where needed. Cut out the pattern pieces.

COWBOY BOOTIES

DIRECTIONS

1 From the tan felt, cut two soles and two booties. From the turquoise felt, cut two cowboy stars and two cowboy bootie bases, pinking the curved upper edges of the bases.

2 Place one bootie base onto the right side of one bootie, matching the center front and lower edges. Topstitch the base in place along the pinked, curved edges, as shown in **Diagram 1.**

Diagram 1

3 With matching thread, top stitch a turquoise star on the outside ankle of the bootie. Sew a length of rickrack about ¼ inch from the top edge of the bootie.

4 Use the awl to punch two holes for the back ankle tie, as marked by the circle on the pattern.

5 With the right sides together, sew the center front seam of the bootie from the toe to the front ankle. Clip the seam at the instep.

6 With the right sides together, sew the sole to the lower edge of the bootie, as shown in **Diagram 2,** matching the toe to the center front seam and the heel to the center back of the bootie. Turn the bootie right side out.

Diagram 2

7 Thread a 12-inch length of gold cording through the holes at the heel. Tie the ends in a bow.

8 Repeat Steps 2 through 7 for the other bootie, topstitching the turquoise star on the opposite side of the ankle.

SANTA BOOTIES

DIRECTIONS

1 From the red felt, cut two soles and two booties. From the white fake fur, cut two 2½ × 8½-inch strips.

2 Place the right side of one long edge of a fur strip to the wrong side of the top edge of the bootie. Using a ¼-inch seam allowance, sew the two edges together. Fold the fur cuff to the right side of the bootie. With the right sides together, sew the center front seam from the toe to the front ankle, catching the ends of the fur cuff in the seam. Clip the seam at the instep.

3 With the right sides together, sew the sole to the lower edge of the bootie, as shown in **Diagram 2** of "Cowboy Booties." Be sure to match the toe to the center front seam and the heel to the center back of the bootie. Then turn the bootie right side out.

4 Cut the ribbon in half. Tack the center of one length to the instep area of the center front seam. Tie the ribbon ends in a bow at the back of the heel.

5 Repeat Steps 2 through 4 for the other bootie.

ELF BOOTIES

MATERIALS

❋ 9 × 11½-inch pieces of felt:
  3 green and 1 red
❋ Red satin ribbons: 48-inch
  length of ⅜-inch-wide and
  24-inch length of ¼-inch-wide

DIRECTIONS

1 From the green felt, cut two soles and two elf booties, pinking the center front seam edges as indicated by the dotted line on the pattern. From the red felt, cut eight hearts.

2 Topstitch an upside-down felt heart to the wrong side of each upper edge point of the bootie, as shown in the **Cuff Diagram.** (The upper edge of the bootie will be turned down for the cuff so the embellishment on the wrong side will be on the right side of the bootie once it is turned.)

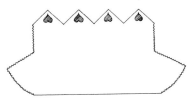

Cuff Diagram

3 Use the awl to punch a hole at each side of the toe for the elf bows, as marked by the small circle on the pattern.

4 With the wrong sides together, sew the center front seam of the bootie.

5 Turn the bootie wrong side out. With the right sides together, sew the sole to the lower edge of the bootie, as shown in **Diagram 2** of "Cowboy Booties" on page 48. Be sure to match the toe to the center front seam and the heel to the center back of the bootie. Turn right side out.

6 Cut the ⅜-inch-wide ribbon in half. Tack the center of one length of ribbon to the instep area of the center front seam. Tie the ribbon ends in a bow at the back of the heel. Fold the cuff down over the ribbon.

7 Cut the ¼-inch-wide ribbon in half. Thread the ribbon through the toe holes. Tie the ribbon ends in a small bow.

8 Repeat Steps 2 through 7 for the other bootie.

HUNTER'S BOOTIES

MATERIALS

❋ 9 × 11½-inch pieces of felt:
  2 green and 2 tan
❋ Large-eyed needle
❋ 2 yards of yellow soutache braid

DIRECTIONS

1 From the green felt, cut two soles and two booties. From the tan felt, cut two hunter's bootie tops, pinking the top edges.

2 Place the tan bootie top onto the right side of the bootie, matching the center front edges. Topstitch the tan top in place along the upper and lower edges.

3 Use the awl to punch the three lacing holes on each center front edge and the two holes for the back ankle tie, as marked by the small circles on the pattern.

4 With the right sides together, sew the center front seam of the bootie from the toe to the front ankle. Clip the seam at the instep.

5 With the right sides together, sew the sole to the lower edge of the boot, as shown in **Diagram 2** of "Cowboy Booties" on page 48. Be sure to match the toe to the center front seam and the heel to the center back of the boot. Turn the bootie right side out.

6 Use the large-eyed needle to thread a 12-inch length of yellow braid through the two holes punched at the heel. Tie the braid ends in a bow.

7 Lace a 24-inch length of braid through the holes on either side of the center front seam, tying the braid ends in a bow at the top, as shown in the photograph on page 47.

8 Repeat Steps 2 through 7 for the other bootie.

BALLET SLIPPERS

MATERIALS

❋ 9 × 11½-inch pieces of felt:
  2 each of white and pink
❋ 18-inch length of 1-inch-wide
  white ruffled eyelet
❋ 2 yards of ⅜-inch-wide pink
  satin ribbon

DIRECTIONS

1 From the pink felt, cut two soles and two ballet slippers. From the white felt, cut two socks.

2 Place a slipper piece onto the right side of the sock piece, matching the center front edges. Topstitch the slipper in place along the upper and toe hole edges; then topstitch a length of eyelet, with the ruffled edge up, along the upper edge of the sock, as shown in the **Topstitching Diagram.**

Topstitching Diagram

3 With the right sides together, sew the center front seam. Clip the seam at the instep.

4 With the right sides together, sew the sole to the lower edge of the bootie, matching the toe to the center front seam and the heel to the center back of the bootie. Turn right side out.

5 Cut the ribbon in half. Tack the center of one length to the slipper heel. Wrap the ribbon ends around the sock, crisscrossing it in the front. Bring the ribbon ends back to the heel and tie a bow.

6 Repeat Steps 1 through 5 for the other slipper.

SADDLE SHOE BOOTIES

MATERIALS

* 9 × 11½-inch pieces of felt: 3 white, 2 black, and 1 light blue
* 1½ yards of narrow red rickrack
* 24-inch length of ⅜-inch-wide red satin ribbon
* Large-eyed needle
* 1 yard of ¹⁄₁₆-inch-wide white satin ribbon

DIRECTIONS

1 From the white felt, cut two soles and two socks. From the black felt, cut four saddle shoe saddles and two saddle shoe heels, pinking the curved edges. From the light blue felt, cut four 1½-inch squares for the argyles.

2 Place one blue square, angled as a diamond, on either edge of the white sock, about ¼ inch from the upper edge and 1½ inches from the center front. Topstitch the squares in place. Sew two 3-inch lengths of rickrack across each square, intersecting at the center. Then sew a length of rickrack along the top edge of the sock, as shown in the **Argyle Diagram.**

Argyle Diagram

3 Use black thread to sew a stitching line where marked by the horizontal dashed line on the pattern to create the illusion of the top of a shoe. Place the two black saddle pieces onto the right side of the sock piece, matching the center front edges. Place the one black heel in the center back of the sock, with the lower edges even. Topstitch the pieces in place along the pinked edges.

4 Use the awl to punch the three lacing holes on each center front edge and the two holes for the back ankle tie, as marked by the small circles on the pattern.

5 With the right sides together, sew the center front seam from the toe to the front ankle. Clip the seam at the instep.

6 With the right sides together, sew the sole to the lower edge of the bootie, matching the toe to the center front seam and the heel to the center back of the bootie. Turn right side out.

7 Cut the ⅜-inch-wide ribbon in half. Use the large-eyed needle to thread a length of ribbon through the two holes punched at the heel. Tie the ends in a bow.

8 Cut the ¹⁄₁₆-inch-wide ribbon in half. Then lace one length of the ribbon through the holes on either side of the center front seam, and tie the ribbon ends in a bow at the top, as shown in the photograph on page 47.

9 Repeat Steps 2 through 8 for the other bootie.

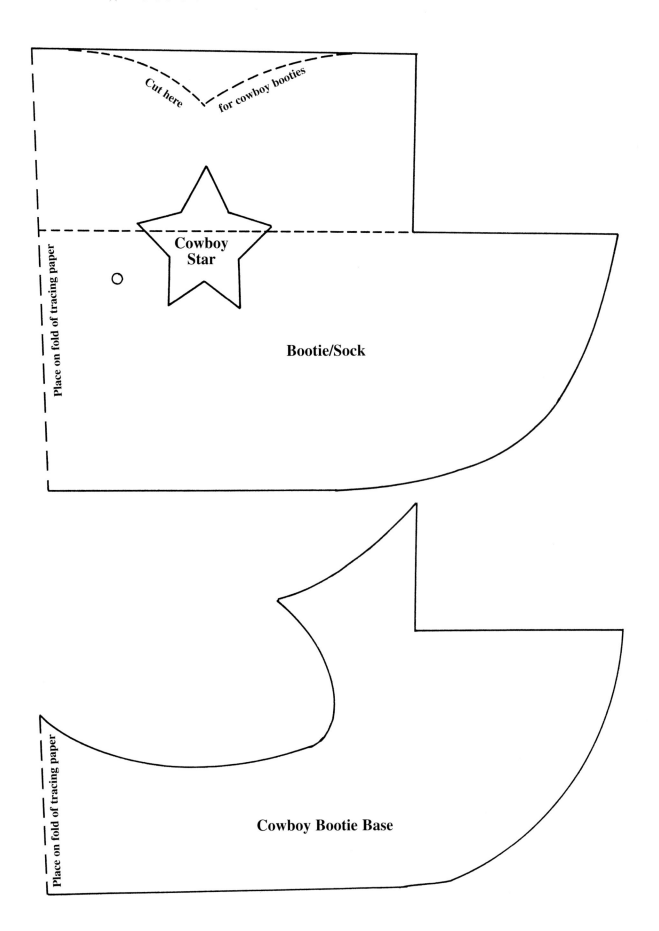

Cut here   for cowboy booties

Cowboy
Star

Place on fold of tracing paper

Bootie/Sock

Cowboy Bootie Base

Place on fold of tracing paper

Heart

Elf Bootie

Place on fold of tracing paper

Ballet Slipper

Place on fold of
tracing paper

Gifts for Adults

*R*emember Mom and Dad, Grandma and Grandpa, and other special family members with handcrafted gifts made with love. For Mom, craft a jewelry piece from elegant beads or a useful trivet from her favorite color crockery. Keep Dad cozy with a warm, knitted scarf or a handsome pillow for his den. Surprise Grandma or Grandpa with personalized mementos like a family tree paper cutting or a one-of-a-kind sweatshirt.

OLD TIES, NEW PILLOWS

*D*ad's favorite, worn ties can begin life anew as a rich silk pillow for the den or family room.

Who would guess that these opulent accents were recycled from no-longer-used cravats?

You might use fabric created from ties to cover the top of a footstool or hassock

as well. Just be sure you cut up ties that Dad no longer wears!

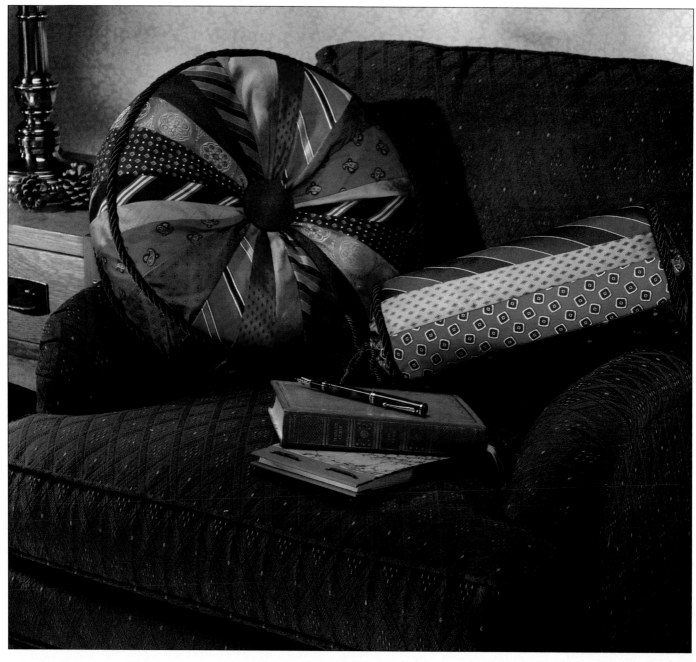

ROUND PILLOW

Size: 16-inch diameter

MATERIALS

❋ Scissors
❋ 11 neckties
❋ Sewing thread
❋ Air-soluble marking pen
❋ Ruler
❋ Iron
❋ Pencil and string
❋ Large sheet of paper
❋ ½ yard of muslin
❋ ½ yard of fabric for the pillow back
❋ Dressmaking pins
❋ 3 yards of decorative upholstery cording with a seam allowance
❋ Polyester fiberfill
❋ 2⅝-inch cover button
❋ Hand-sewing needle

DIRECTIONS

1 Slit open the ties along the back seam. Remove the interfacings, linings, and tags.

2 Beginning at the wide end of each tie, and in this order, cut 6-inch, 9-inch, 6-inch, and 9-inch pieces, as shown in **Diagram 1.** Place the 9-inch pieces in one pile and the 6-inch pieces in another pile.

9"

6"

9"

6"

Diagram 1

3 Unfold the ties and press them flat. Mark the 9-inch pieces first. Mark the center of each narrow end, then mark ½ inch on either side of the center mark. At the widest end of each piece, place a mark ¼ inch outside the original fold lines of the tie. Connect the marks on each side and cut along them to trim off the excess, as shown by the dashed lines in **Diagram 2.**

½"

½"

Diagram 2

4 With right sides facing and using a ¼-inch seam allowance, sew the 9-inch strips together along the long edges to form a circle, placing the narrow end of each strip at the same edge, as shown in **Diagram 3;** do not sew the last seam. Press the seams in the same direction.

Diagram 3

5 Sew a line of gathering stitches ½ inch and ⅜ inch from the edge along the narrow ends of the sewn strips. Sew the last seam together to form a circle. Pull the gathers tightly and flatten the ring to shape the center of the pillow front. Tie the thread ends securely.

6 Referring to "Simple Compasses for Large Circles" on page 58 and using the pencil and string, make a compass and outline a 16½-inch-diameter circle on a large sheet of paper. Use this pattern to cut one circle each of muslin and fabric for the pillow back.

Tips for Ties

❊

If Dad doesn't have enough ties in complementary colors to create a good-looking pillow, choose a couple of his that look great together and take them with you to thrift or consignment shops. You should be able to purchase several ties for a dollar or two. You could also shop the local flea markets for bargains. Dry cleaners frequently have unclaimed ties that they are willing to sell inexpensively.

❊

When cutting the ties, avoid using the "knot" areas as these areas are most likely to be soiled and stretched out of shape.

❊

If a tie is soiled, you may wish to wash it. Hand wash it carefully in a gentle detergent or dishwashing liquid, roll it in a towel to remove any excess moisture, and dry flat. Always handle ties carefully as the fabric has been cut on the bias, and it can be stretched out of shape, especially when wet.

7 Pin the pillow front, right side up, onto the muslin circle. Trim off the excess outer ends of the ties. Carefully baste the ties to the circle approximately ½ inch from the outside edge.

8 Using ¼-inch seam allowances, sew the 6-inch tie pieces together in a strip long enough to go around the circumference of the pillow front. When sewing the pieces together, match the color sequence of the tie patterns in the strip with those in the pillow front, and match the wide ends with the wider strips and the narrow ends with those in the narrower strips. If necessary, trim each end to the width of the corresponding strip of the pillow top, including the ¼-inch seam allowance.

9 Cut a strip of muslin 6 inches wide and long enough to fit around the circumference of the pillow front, plus 1 inch for the seam allowances. Pin the tie strip, right side up, onto the muslin strip. Trim off any excess tie ends. Baste the pieces together ½ inch from each long edge of the strip. Sew the narrow ends of the strip together to form a ring, leaving approximately a 2½-inch opening in the seam for turning the pillow. This piece is the pillow side.

10 Baste the upholstery cording along the seam line on the right side of the pillow front and back. With wrong sides facing each other, sew the edges of the pillow side to the pillow front. Sew the opposite edge of the pillow side to the pillow back, matching the order of ties on the pillow top. Turn the pillow right side out and stuff it with the polyester fiberfill to the desired firmness.

11 Cover the button with fabric and hand sew it to the center of the pillow, stitching through the entire pillow to anchor it in place.

Simple Compasses for Large Circles

Tie one end of the string to the pencil. Stretching the string taut, tie a knot near the opposite end of the string so that the distance between the point of the upright pencil and the knot is exactly half the diameter (the radius) desired. Insert a pushpin into the newly tied knot, then stick the pin in the center of the paper. Holding the pencil upright and stretching the string taut, swing the pencil around to outline a circle.

You can also make a large compass by cutting a strip of lightweight cardboard slightly longer than half the desired diameter of the circle. Draw a line that is half the diameter of the circle (the radius) down the center of the strip. Place a pin through the cardboard at one end of the line. Punch a hole through the cardboard at the other end of the line. Use the pin end of the strip for the center of the circle and place it in the center of a piece of paper. Place the point of a pencil through the punched hole at the other end. Rotate the pencil, drawing a circle.

NECK ROLL

Size: 13 inches long

MATERIALS

❋ Scissors
❋ 9 neckties
❋ Ruler
❋ Air-soluble marking pen
❋ ½ yard muslin
❋ Iron
❋ Dressmaker pins
❋ Sewing thread
❋ 1¼ yards of decorative upholstery cording with a seam allowance
❋ Two 7-inch-diameter matching fabric circles to line the pillow ends
❋ 2 yards of ⅜-inch-wide cording
❋ Four 3-inch long tassels to match the cording
❋ Fabric glue
❋ Polyester fiberfill

DIRECTIONS

1 Slit open the ties along the back seam. Remove the interfacings, linings, and tags.

2 Beginning at the widest point of the wider end of each tie, cut 5-inch, 15-inch, and 5-inch pieces, as shown in **Diagram 1.**

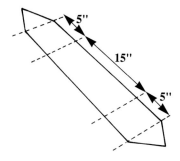

Diagram 1

3 Unfold the ties and press them flat. Mark the 15-inch pieces first. Mark ¼ inch outside the original fold lines of the tie. Connect the marks on each side; cut along them to trim off the excess, referring to **Diagram 2** of the "Round Pillow" on page 57.

4 Cut a 15 × 21-inch piece of muslin. Pin one 15-inch tie strip, right side up, onto the muslin at one narrow end. Place a second tie strip face down on top of the first, but facing in the opposite direction, lining up the edges on one side. Using a ¼-inch seam allowance, sew the ties to the muslin along the long inner edge of the tie strips, as shown in **Diagram 2.**

Diagram 2

5 Open the second tie strip right side up and press it flat. Baste the other long edge of the first tie strip to the muslin, as shown in **Diagram 3.**

Diagram 3

6 Place a third tie strip, face down and reversing direction again, on top of the second strip, matching the long edges. Sew the ties to the muslin along the long

inner edge of the tie strips. Open out the third strip and press it flat. Continue to sew the remaining long strips in this way until the muslin piece is covered. Trim the piece to 13½ × 19½ inches. Using a ½-inch seam allowance, baste around all edges of the joined tie fabric to secure it to the muslin. With right sides facing each other, use a ½-inch seam allowance to sew the 15-inch-long edges of the piece together to form a tube.

7 To make the pillow ends, cut two 6 × 21-inch pieces of muslin. On each piece of muslin, sew the 5-inch tie strips together in the same order as on the larger piece, trimming them to the width of the corresponding 15-inch tie piece but adding a ½-inch seam allowance before cutting. (Cut these pieces straight. Disregard the tie's original fold lines.) Pay strict attention to the order in which each strip is sewn to the muslin so that each end matches the corresponding edge of the tube. Trim the completed sewn piece to 4 × 19½ inches.

8 To form a tube, sew the narrow ends of each pillow end together, right sides facing, with a ½-inch seam allowance and leaving the last 1 inch of the outer end of the seam open for a casing opening, as shown in **Diagram 4.** Press the seam open and topstitch close to the folded edges of the casing opening.

Diagram 4

9 Press under ¼ inch, then ½ inch along the casing edge. Topstitch the casing edge in place, as shown in **Diagram 5.**

Diagram 5

10 Baste the upholstery cording on the right side and along the seam line on each end of the larger pillow tube. With right sides together, use a ¼-inch seam allowance to sew the pillow end tubes to the larger pillow tube. With the right side facing out, sew one of the fabric circles to the seam allowance at one end of the larger pillow tube. Turn the pillow right side out.

11 Cut the narrow twisted cording in half and thread one length through the casing on each pillow end tube. Tie a tassel 1 inch from each end of the cord. Fold up the cord end and glue it in place. Wrap matching thread around the cording to cover the glued end. Pull the twisted cord on the fabric-lined end to gather the pillow end. Tie the cord into a knotted bow. Stuff the neck roll with polyester fiberfill.

12 Hand sew the other fabric circle inside the remaining pillow end. Insert the cord and tie a tassel 1 inch from each end of the cord. Fold the cord end and glue it in place. Wrap matching thread around the cording to cover the glued end. Pull the cord to gather the second fabric end and tie it in a bow.

DAD'S HOLIDAY MUFFLER

*K*nit one, purl two" goes the
old expression. Simply reverse that
to "Knit two, purl one," and you
have memorized the super-simple
pattern stitch for this wonderful scarf.
Each and every row is the same, so it
works up in a wink. Be sure to knit
more than one since Dad's not the
only one who would enjoy its
colorful warmth in winter!

★

Size: About 11 × 48 inches,
including fringe

MATERIALS

❋ Four 3-ounce/85-gram balls of
   Lion Brand Wool-Ease Sprinkles
   worsted-weight yarn*
❋ Pair of size 8 knitting needles
❋ Scissors
❋ 6-inch square of cardboard
❋ Size G or H crochet hook

See the "Buyer's Guide" on page 176.

DIRECTIONS

CHECKING THE GAUGE

To make sure the finished size will be
correct, take the time to check your
gauge. Here we are using a gauge of 14
stitches = 2 inches. (See "Checking
Gauge" on the opposite page for additional information.)

MAKING THE HOLIDAY MUFFLER

1 Begin the muffler by casting on
72 stitches.

2 Row 1: * Knit 2 stitches, purl 1
stitch; repeat these 3 stitches
from the * across all the stitches on
the needle.

3 Repeat Row 1 for the pattern until the muffler is 42 inches long. Bind off in pattern.

KNOTTING THE FRINGE

1 Use the cardboard square to measure and then cut the yarn strands for the fringe. (See "How to Make Fringe" on this page.)

2 Use four strands of yarn for each fringe. Knot a fringe in the first stitch, then in every third stitch across each narrow end of the muffler.

How to Make Fringe

1. Wrap yarn around a piece of cardboard and cut the loops at one edge, as shown in Diagram 1.

Diagram 1

2. Fold four of the cut yarn strands in half. Insert the crochet hook into an edge stitch and pull the folded yarn ends through, as shown in Diagram 2.

Diagram 2

3. While the folded yarn is still on the hook, pick up the yarn ends and pull them through the loops, as shown in Diagram 3. Pull the yarn ends to tighten the knot.

Diagram 3

4. After all the fringe is knotted across the edge, trim the ends even, as shown in Diagram 4.

Diagram 4

Checking Gauge

Gauge is the number of stitches and rows per inch. You can change your gauge depending on the needle or hook size and the yarn you are using, as well as how tightly or loosely you knit or crochet. In order for a garment to fit properly, it is essential that your gauge matches the one given in the instructions. Even if you are knitting or crocheting an item for which fit is not an issue, gauge is still very important. The way the completed project feels—referred to as the "hand"—depends on the gauge. If your gauge is too tight, your piece will be stiff as a board. If the gauge is too loose, your piece will be limp and uneven. Even if you want to get started right away on the project you have planned, take time to check your gauge.

❊

To make sure the finished size of the knit piece will be correct, check the knitting for the proper gauge. You may want to knit a sample swatch, or a few inches of the item to test the gauge. Referring to the diagram below, use a ruler to measure horizontally across a row to determine the number of stitches per inch. Don't measure the first row of knitting; your tension may be tighter than normal when you first start to knit. Measure vertically along the side of the stitches to determine the number of rows per inch. Change your needle size if your gauge is incorrect: Use a larger needle if the knitting has too many stitches and rows per inch, or a smaller needle if the knitting has not enough stitches and rows per inch. Knit another swatch until you obtain the correct gauge.

TIME FOR BEADS JEWELRY

Use dramatic beads in rich patterns to produce timely jewelry such as this elegant wristwatch, pendant watch, and eyeglass chain. Or give new life to an old watch by adding one of these unique beaded bands.

ADJUSTABLE BEADED WATCHBAND

Size: Adjustable

MATERIALS

❋ Scissors
❋ Ruler
❋ 48-inch length of ¹⁄₃₂-inch diameter elastic beading cord
❋ 30 spacers
❋ Extra large face watch with ¾-inch pins
❋ Thick white craft glue
❋ 16 small beads
❋ 6 medium beads
❋ 11 large beads
❋ 6 jump rings
❋ 3 charms
All beads and jewelry findings used here are from The Beadery.*
Use the **Bead Identification** chart on the opposite page to assist in bead selection.

See the "Buyer's Guide" on page 176.

DIRECTIONS

1 Cut a 16-inch length of cord, then string on the first bead in Pattern A, as shown in **Diagram 1.**

Thread cord through center bead, then repeat pattern in the reverse order

Diagram 1

2 Working from front to back, thread the cord around the lower watch pin. Securely knot the cord ¼ inch after the bead, as shown in **Diagram 2.** Put a dab of glue on the knot and trim the cord end. The knot should be tucked into the adjacent bead.

Diagram 2

3 Referring to **Diagram 1,** string the rest of Pattern A and the large center bead (a filigree puff disc on the **Bead Identification** chart), then repeat Pattern A in the reverse order.

4 Working from front to back, thread the cord around the watch pin on the opposite side of the watch face. Estimate the size of the recipient's wrist or try the watch on; add or subtract beads to adjust the length to fit. Make a knot around the last bead as in Step 1.

5 Repeat Steps 1 through 3 twice more as follows: String Pattern B beads first and then Pattern C beads, as shown in **Diagrams 1** and **3**, threading each

cord through the large single center bead before reversing the order of the beads.

Diagram 3

6 Using two jump rings, attach each of the three charms randomly on the watchband.

BEADED WATCH PENDANT

Size: 30 inches long with a 3-inch pendant

DIRECTIONS

Note: If space allows for decorating pins, remove the upper pin from the watch and string three 4mm gold beads onto the pin. Replace the pin in the watch.

1 Wrap one end of the 40-inch length of monofilament thread around the top watch pin and tie a

Bead Identification

This chart shows beads grouped roughly by size to help you make substitutions if needed. Make sure you select beading cord that will fit through any small-hole beads used. When stringing large-hole beads on thin beading cord, use a tapered spacer (rondelle or mushroom bead) before and after to hold them in place.

SPACERS	SMALL	MEDIUM	LARGE
6mm Floral Rondelle Bead	4mm Round Bead	10mm Round Bead (Large Hole)	13 × 12.5mm Athenian Bead (Large Hole)
6mm Rondelle Bead	6mm Round Bead	10mm Melon Bead (Large Hole)	14 × 10mm Oval Bead (Large Hole)
7mm Floral Ring	7mm Round Bead	10mm Nugget (Large Hole)	18 × 8mm Rectangle Bead (Large Hole)
7 × 6mm Mushroom Bead	9 × 8mm Mushroom Bead		
8mm Ring	6mm Faceted Bead 6mm Sand Bead	10mm Faceted Bead (Large Hole)	18 × 8.5mm Filigree Puff Disc (Large Hole)
10mm Disc (Lg. Hole)			
8mm Corrugated Ring	8 × 6mm Drum Bead (Large Hole) 8mm Cube Bead (Large Hole)		

secure knot. Put a dab of glue on the knot to completely secure it.

2 Thread a beading needle onto the long end of the monofilament thread. String a small mushroom bead and floral rondelle, as shown in **Diagram 1.** String the beads, as shown in the **Necklace Pattern,** six times.

Diagram 1

3 Repeat the necklace pattern again, omitting the last nine beads. String a floral rondelle bead and a small mushroom bead.

4 Referring to **Diagram 2,** thread the needle around the top watch pin. Make sure that all the beads are nestled together, then tie a secure knot. Put a dab of glue on the knot. Feed the ends back through the adjacent beads. Trim.

Diagram 2

5 String **Pin Pattern A** onto a head pin. Use the wire cutters to trim the pin to ⅜ inch. Referring

to **Diagram 3,** make a loop at the end of a pin, using the round-nose pliers to form the loop. Repeat this step to make a second **Pin Pattern A** and one **Pin Pattern B.**

Trim end

Bend end

Form and close loop

Diagram 3

6 Remove the lower watch pin. String the three head pin loops alternately with two 4mm gold beads onto the watch pin, as shown in **Diagram 4.** Replace the pin in the watch.

Diagram 4

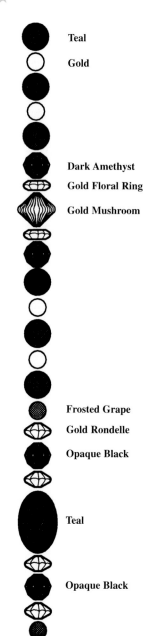

Necklace Pattern

Teal
Gold
Gold
Teal
Dark Amethyst
Gold Floral Ring
Gold Mushroom

Frosted Grape
Gold Rondelle
Opaque Black

Teal

Opaque Black

Pin Pattern A

Opaque Black
Gold
Frosted Grape
Gold Rondelle
Teal

Frosted Grape

Gold

Gold Mushroom

Gold Rondelle

Dark Amethyst

Pin Pattern B

BEADED WATCHBAND

Size: 7¼-inch total length

DIRECTIONS

1 Attach the connector findings to the watch by removing one of the pins and sliding one of the connector findings onto it. Compress the pin and replace it on the watch, making sure the connector is attached right side out. Repeat for the second connector.

2 Use the wire cutters to cut a 20-inch length of tiger tail. This length will make a watchband with 2 inches of beads on either side of the face. If desired, this length and the number of beads strung on the wire can be adjusted. Insert one end of the wire into one of the outside holes of a connector finding and pull about 6 inches through the hole. Then string a crimp bead onto the wire. Thread the short end of the wire around and through the crimp bead a second time, as shown in **Diagram 1.** Pull the wire tight and use the pliers or crimp bead tool to securely crimp the bead onto the wire near the end. Trim the excess wire close to the bead.

Diagram 1

3 Pull the wire until the crimp bead is snugly inside the connector finding. String **Pattern A** beads, as shown on page 66. Referring to **Diagram 2,** thread the wire into an outside hole of the

clasp and out through the center hole, making sure the clasp is attached right side out. String **Pattern B** beads, as shown on page 66, then insert the wire into the center hole of the connector finding and out the last hole. String **Pattern A** beads, inserting the wire into the last hole of the clasp and pulling the wire to remove all but 1/16 inch slack on each bead strand. String a crimp bead. Thread the wire around and through the bead a second time and crimp the bead as close to the clasp as possible. Trim the end.

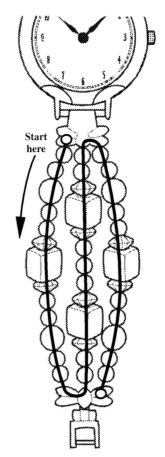

Start here

Diagram 2

4 Repeat Steps 2 and 3 of the beading procedure for the other side of the watch face.

5 Make sure the trimmed wire ends are tucked inside the connectors then fill the backs of the connectors and clasps with glue.

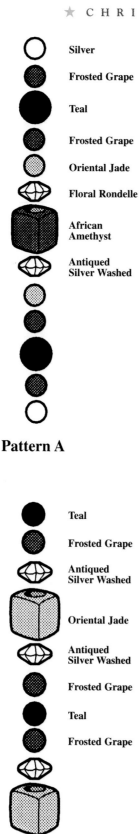

Silver

Frosted Grape

Teal

Frosted Grape

Oriental Jade

Floral Rondelle

African Amethyst

Antiqued Silver Washed

Pattern A

BEADED EYEGLASS HOLDER

Size: 29 inches long

MATERIALS

❊ 40-inch length of gold tiger tail (plastic-coated twisted wire)
❊ Jeweler's pliers and wire cutters
❊ 2 double-bead gold-tone tips
❊ 2 gold-tone eyeglass holders
❊ 6mm round beads: 48 African Amethyst
❊ 4mm round beads: 16 Frosted Grape, 14 Opaque Black, and 32 in 24K Gold Washed
❊ 6mm floral rondelle beads: 30 Antique 24K Gold Washed
❊ 8mm cube beads with a large hole: 8 Oriental Jade
❊ 14 × 10mm oval beads with a large hole: 7 Teal
❊ Straight pin or needle
All beads and jewelry findings used here are from The Beadery.* Use the **Bead Identification** chart on page 63 to assist in bead selection.

See the "Buyer's Guide" on page 176.

DIRECTIONS

1 Tie a double overhand knot near one end of the tiger tail. Trim the excess wire close to the knot. Thread the long end of the wire through the hole in a bead tip so the knot rests in the cup, as shown in **Diagram 1.**

Diagram 1

2 Close the bead tip cup, hiding the knot. Close the loop of the bead tip around the loop in an eyeglass holder, as shown in **Diagram 2.**

Diagram 2

3 String **Pattern A** beads, as shown below, onto the wire seven times. Then string **Pattern A** beads onto the wire once more, omitting the last five beads.

4 String on a bead tip, as shown in **Diagram 3.** Remove all but ⅛ inch of slack from the beaded wire. Tie an overhand knot in the wire, sliding the knot into the cup of the bead tip and using the tip of a pin or needle to work the knot along the wire. Trim off the excess wire.

Diagram 3

5 Repeat Step 2 to finish the eyeglass holder strand.

African Amethyst
Antiqued Gold

Frosted Grape
Floral Rondelle
Oriental Jade

Opaque Black

Teal

Pattern A

Teal

Frosted Grape

Antiqued Silver Washed

Oriental Jade

Antiqued Silver Washed

Frosted Grape

Teal

Frosted Grape

Frosted Grape

Teal

Pattern B

NAVAJO BOOKMARK

Size: 2½ × 9¼ inches

MATERIALS

❋ Pencil
❋ Dressmaker's tracing paper
❋ Ultrasuede synthetic suede: one 10 × 6-inch piece of cream, one 2½ × 9-inch piece of coffee, one 2½ × 8-inch piece of taupe, and one 1 × 7-inch piece of turquoise*
❋ Tracing wheel
❋ Scissors and pinking shears
❋ Water-soluble marking pen
❋ Ruler
❋ Fabric glue

See the "Buyer's Guide" on page 176.

DIRECTIONS

1 Trace the **Navajo Bookmark Patterns** on this page onto the tracing paper, outlining the shape for each color area as a separate pattern. You will have one each of the A, B, and C patterns, and three each of the D, E, and F patterns.

2 Mark the pattern shapes on the wrong sides of the Ultrasuede pieces as follows: Begin by placing the dressmaker's tracing paper on the wrong side of the fabric, marking side down. Position the pattern shape on top of the dressmaker's tracing paper. Roll the tracing wheel along the outlines of the pattern to mark the shape onto the fabric.

3 Cut out all the pieces, using the pinking shears to cut out the A piece and the three D pieces to create a decorative edge.

4 Use the marking pen and ruler to mark 1½-inch-long lines at the bottom end of the A piece, spac-

ing the lines ⅛ inch apart. Mark on the wrong side of the fabric. Cut along the marked lines for the fringe.

5 Glue the fabric pieces together, layering them as follows: Begin with the B piece centered on the fringed A piece. Referring to the **Navajo Bookmark Patterns** for placement, continue to glue each fabric piece in alphabetical order onto the bookmark, ending with the D diamonds, the E diamonds, and the F squares set on point.

Synthetic Suede Savvy

If you don't have synthetic suede leftovers available from your other projects, look for bags of scraps in fabric stores that carry high-fashion fabrics.

Synthetic suede is also sold by the "square." See the "Buyer's Guide" on page 176 for a mail-order source.

The glue you choose for your bookmarks is very important. Be sure to use fabric glue as recommended because most craft glues will cause the synthetic suede to stiffen.

To remove wrinkles and creases from synthetic suede, press the wrong side of the fabric using a press cloth and an iron on the synthetic setting.

Navajo Bookmark Patterns

Chapter Three

Supersaver Gifts

*E*veryone's Christmas list includes people to remember with "just a little something."

Here are penny-wise gifts that cost just a few dollars to craft, time-wise gifts that can be finished

in an hour or less, and eco-wise gifts that are kind to the environment. You'll also find that

many of these gifts can be easily made in multiples for your favorite fund-raising event

or charity. And most are simple enough for children to make.

DRESS-FORM CHATELAINE

*A*ny seamstress or quilt enthusiast on your gift list will be delighted to put this mini-mannequin to work. Designed to keep

sewing aids at hand, this replica of a dressmaker's form holds pins, scissors, and a tape measure. The recipient can

set it on the arm of her chair or close to her sewing machine to keep those easily misplaced small tools nearby.

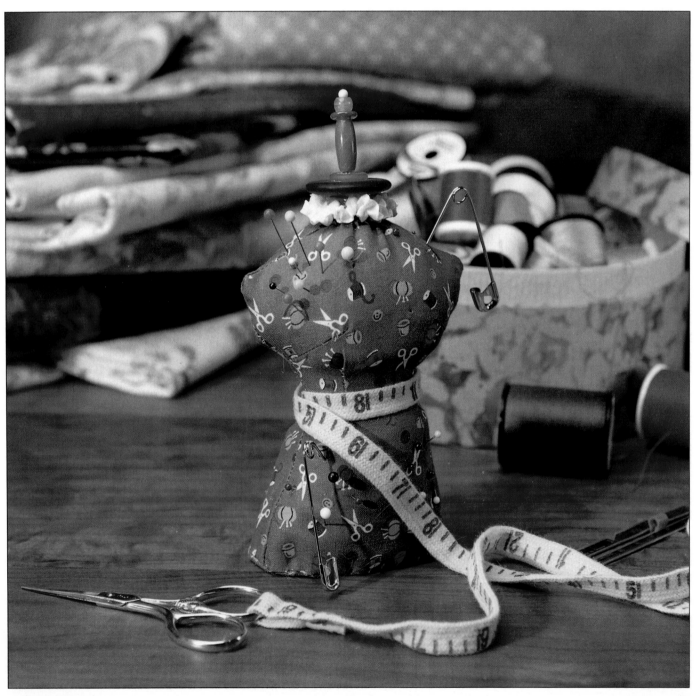

Size: About 6 inches tall

MATERIALS

❋ Pencil
❋ Tracing paper
❋ Scissors
❋ 8 × 10-inch piece of print fabric
❋ Sewing machine
❋ Thread
❋ Polyester fiberfill
❋ Piece of cardboard
❋ Hand-sewing needle
❋ Thick white craft glue
❋ ⅛ yard of white crinkled ribbon
❋ Long straight pin
❋ Assorted color and size beads to
   make the finial, such as a small
   round bead, a small flat bead, an
   oval bead, a medium flat bead,
   and a large flat bead
❋ Miniature tape measure or
   printed tape measure shoelace
❋ Small sewing scissors

DIRECTIONS

1 Trace the dress-form patterns onto the tracing paper. Cut out the pattern pieces. From the print fabric, cut out the front and back dress-forms. Mark the base pattern on the wrong side of the fabric. Add a ½-inch seam allowance to the outer edge and cut out the base piece.

2 Sew the darts in the front and back dress-form pieces. Using a ¼-inch seam allowance, sew the front and back pieces together, leaving the bottom edge of the form open and easing in any fullness along the bust dart. Turn right side out and stuff firmly with the fiberfill. Turn under ½ inch along the open bottom edge.

3 Cut a base piece from the cardboard. Baste around the fabric base piece, ½ inch from the edge. Place the cardboard piece, centered, on the wrong side of the fabric base piece. Pull the basting thread to gather the fabric edges around the cardboard base.

4 Slip stitch the fabric base to the bottom opening of the dress-form, adding more stuffing if needed.

5 Glue the white ribbon around the neck of the dress-form. On the long straight pin, place a small round bead, a small flat bead, an oval bead, a medium flat bead, then a large flat bead, as shown in the photograph on the opposite page. Push the beaded pin into the top of the dress-form, gluing it in place. Tack the tape measure or shoelace around the waist of the dress-form. Thread the other end of the tape measure through one handle of the small scissors, fold the tape measure over, and tack in place.

Base

Back Dress Form

Front Dress Form

Leave open

Place on fold of tracing paper

Place on fold of tracing paper

Leave open

TWINKLING TOES SOCKS

Simple cotton socks are the palette for these creative concoctions. Use tiny bits and pieces of trim left from bigger projects and add bright new ribbons, laces, buttons, and charms to duplicate the snappy socks shown here. Or just use these as inspiration for your own creations. Since socks stretch, you need only a general idea of size to assure a perfect gift.

RED SOCKS

Size: As desired

MATERIALS

* ❋ Scissors
* ❋ 16-inch length of ⅞-inch-wide black-and-white grosgrain ribbon
* ❋ Gold embroidery floss
* ❋ Large-eyed embroidery needle
* ❋ Pair of red socks
* ❋ Four ½-inch, red, star-shaped two-hole buttons

DIRECTIONS

1 Cut the ribbon into four 4-inch lengths. Fold each into a loop, overlapping the ends ¼ inch. Pinch each together in the center to form a bow. Using six strands of floss, tack the loops in place.

2 Referring to the photograph on the opposite page, sew two bows to the outside of each sock cuff. Use the embroidery floss to sew a button in the center of each bow.

GOLD SOCKS

Size: As desired

MATERIALS

* ❋ Air-soluble marking pen
* ❋ Pair of gold socks
* ❋ Gold embroidery floss
* ❋ Large-eyed embroidery needle
* ❋ 32 assorted metallic gold charms

DIRECTIONS

1 Use the pen to mark 16 evenly spaced dots around the cuff edge.

2 Use the embroidery floss to sew a charm at each mark. Refer to the photograph on the opposite page.

PURPLE SOCKS

Size: As desired

MATERIALS

* ❋ Scissors
* ❋ 1 yard of ¾-inch-wide ruffled multicolored lace
* ❋ Purple and red sewing thread
* ❋ Hand-sewing needle
* ❋ Pair of purple socks
* ❋ Pink embroidery floss
* ❋ Large-eyed embroidery needle
* ❋ Heart-shaped buttons: six ⅜-inch light purple and four ¾-inch dark purple with two holes, and eight ¼-inch red shank

DIRECTIONS

1 Cut the lace in half. Using purple thread, sew a row of lace around the edge of each sock cuff, stretching the cuff as you sew and overlapping the raw ends. Sew a second row of lace above the first row.

2 Use the embroidery floss to sew three light purple and two dark purple buttons to the outside of each sock cuff. Referring to the photograph on the opposite page, use the red sewing thread to sew four red buttons to each cuff.

CREAM SOCKS

Size: As desired

MATERIALS

* ❋ Scissors
* ❋ Sewing machine
* ❋ Cream sewing thread
* ❋ 20-inch length of ½-inch-wide white lace
* ❋ Pair of cream socks
* ❋ Shank buttons: twelve ¼- to ⅜-inch half-round pearl, and six assorted size pearl and gold

DIRECTIONS

1 Use a small machine zigzag stitch to sew 10 inches of lace to the lower edge of each sock cuff, stretching the cuff as you sew.

2 Sew six pearl buttons and three of the assorted buttons randomly to the outside of each cuff, as shown in the photograph on the opposite page.

BLUE SOCKS

Size: As desired

MATERIALS

* ❋ Scissors
* ❋ 22-inch length of red grosgrain ribbon with white dots
* ❋ Sewing thread
* ❋ Hand-sewing needle
* ❋ Pair of blue socks
* ❋ Gold, star-shaped shank buttons: two ⅝-inch and two ¹¹⁄₁₆-inch

DIRECTIONS

1 Cut the grosgrain ribbon into four 5½-inch lengths.

2 Run a gathering thread along one long edge of each ribbon length, pulling the thread to gather the ribbon into a rosette and overlapping the ends. Turn under about ⅛ inch on the top ribbon end. Knot the thread to secure the gathers.

3 Sew two ribbon rosettes to the outside of each sock cuff, as shown in the photograph on the opposite page. Sew a button in the center of each rosette, using one large button and one small button on each cuff.

FAIRYLAND FINGER PUPPETS

*G*ive the gift of imagination. This cast of characters is definitely in need of a playwright to bring them to life. Children will have hours of fun spinning yarns and acting out dramatic plays with these simple heroes or heroines. The puppets are cut from craft foam and are so easy you may be inspired to branch out with some variations all your own.

★

Size: Each about 4 inches tall

MATERIALS

❋ Pencil
❋ Tracing paper
❋ Scissors and pinking shears
❋ Fine-point, permanent marking pen
❋ 1 sheet each of craft foam, such as from Westrim Crafts, in light and dark pink, bright and lime green, white, black, gray, red, and yellow*
❋ Craft knife
❋ Thick white craft glue
❋ Toothpicks
❋ Paper punch in ¼-inch and ⅛-inch sizes
❋ Pointed artist's brush
❋ Acrylic paints in white, black, red, and light pink
❋ 2 yards of yellow yarn
See the "Buyer's Guide" on page 176.

DIRECTIONS

BASIC DIRECTIONS FOR ALL THE PUPPETS

1 Use the tracing paper to trace each piece of the finger puppet patterns, including a puppet base, on the opposite page and page 84. Make a pattern piece for each colored section of the puppet, extending the piece if needed where a shape might overlap. A separate pattern is provided for the fairy's dress. The dashed lines on the patterns indicate where pieces overlap. The smaller circles, such as the eyes and cheeks, will be cut out with the paper punches, so a pattern piece is not necessary. Other pattern details

will be painted. No pattern is needed for the fairy's hair; it will be braided from yarn. Cut out the individual pattern pieces.

2 Use the fine-point permanent marking pen to outline each pattern piece on the wrong side of the craft foam. Refer to the photograph on this page or the specific assembly instructions for the color of each piece.

3 Cut out each foam piece using the scissors for smooth edges, and the pinking shears for zigzag edges, such as the fairy and frog crowns and the fairy apron. Use the craft knife to cut the finger slit in the puppet base.

"BROWN BAG IT" PAPER JEWELRY

*E*xamine this wonderful gift jewelry and consider its humble beginnings—brown paper

bags and torn scraps of magazine photos! The simple shapes are easy to duplicate,

and we bet it will be one of your easiest craft projects this holiday season.

We added metallic beads on each piece for a glittering contrast.

MATERIALS

For all the bracelets:
❋ Ruler
❋ Scissors
❋ Disposable gloves
❋ Foam brush
❋ Plaid Enterprise's Mod Podge glue-type finishing sealer*
❋ Large sewing needle
❋ Needle-nose and flat-nose pliers
❋ Wire cutters
*See the "Buyer's Guide" on page 176.

PLEATED-PAPER BRACELET

Size: As desired

MATERIALS

❋ Brown Kraft paper or grocery bag
❋ Round toothpicks
❋ ½ yard of tiger tail plastic-coated twisted wire
❋ 2 crimp beads
❋ 1 barrel clasp
❋ Twenty-two 8mm faceted beads, such as The Beadery No. 700*
❋ Ten 8mm corrugated disc beads, such as The Beadery No. 856*
*See the "Buyer's Guide" on page 176.

DIRECTIONS

1 To make the paper-tube beads, cut six ½ × 6-inch pieces of Kraft paper. While wearing disposable gloves, brush a thin coat of sealer on both sides of each piece of paper. Begin at one narrow end and wrap each paper piece around a toothpick, forming a tight tube, as shown in **Diagram 1.**

Diagram 1

2 Hold each paper end in place until the sealer sets. When each bead is dry to the touch on the surface but not yet hard, gently twist the toothpick to remove it from the bead. Use the center hole of each bead for stringing. Apply a second coat of sealer to the outer surface. Let it dry thoroughly. Repeat to make six small paper-tube beads.

3 To make the pleated-paper beads, cut five ½ × 6-inch pieces of Kraft paper. To crease the paper for pleating, fold each piece in half crosswise. Fold each half twice more, creasing each fold sharply so the piece is finally folded into eight sections, as shown in **Diagram 2.**

Diagram 2

4 Open out the paper strip and coat both sides of each paper with the sealer, making sure to wear disposable gloves. Refold each strip into the accordion shape. Hold the folded paper together until the sealer sets and keeps it together in the center. Use the large needle to punch a hole through the center of the pleats for stringing. Apply a second coat of the sealer to the outer surface. Let it dry thoroughly. Repeat this step to make five pleated-paper beads.

5 Using the large needle, string the tiger tail through one crimp bead, through the loop on one side of the clasp, and back through the crimp bead, as shown in

Diagram 3. Flatten the crimp bead with the needle-nose pliers to fasten the clasp on the wire.

Diagram 3

6 Thread a faceted bead on the tiger tail. Refer to **Diagram 4** to string the next bead sequence. Referring to the photograph on page 91, continue to string this sequence for the remaining beads; end with a faceted bead.

Diagram 4

7 Fasten the other side of the clasp and the second crimp bead in the same way as in Step 5. Trim the excess tiger tail.

TUBE-BEAD BRACELET

Size: As desired

DIRECTIONS

1 To make the paper-tube beads, cut six ½ × 6-inch pieces of Kraft paper. While wearing disposable gloves, brush a thin coat of sealer on both sides of each piece of paper. Begin at one narrow end and wrap each paper piece around a toothpick, forming a tight tube, as shown in **Diagram 1** of "Pleated-Paper Bracelet" on the opposite page.

2 Hold each paper end in place until the sealer sets. When each bead is dry to the touch on the surface but not yet hard, gently twist the toothpick to remove it from the bead. Use the center hole of each bead for stringing. Apply a second coat of sealer to the outer surface. Let it dry thoroughly. Repeat to make six small paper-tube beads.

3 Using the large needle, string the tiger tail through one crimp bead, through the loop on one side of the clasp, and back through the crimp bead, as shown in **Diagram 3** of "Pleated-Paper Bracelet." Flatten the crimp bead with the needle-nose pliers to fasten the clasp on the wire.

4 Using the pliers and referring to the **Stringing Diagram** for the bead sequence, use the large needle to string the beads on the tiger tail. End with a disc, fluted beads, and a disc.

Stringing Diagram

5 Fasten the other side of the clasp and the second crimp bead in the same way as at the beginning. Trim the excess tiger tail.

COLORED-PAPER BRACELET

Size: As desired

DIRECTIONS

1 Tear the colored paper into small pieces.

2 While wearing disposable gloves and holding the bead on a wooden skewer, brush a thin coat of sealer over the surface of the wooden bead. Press the torn paper pieces onto the surface of the bead, working from the center out to the edges. Use your fingers to smooth the paper around the curves and to eliminate any bubbles. Add layers of paper pieces, overlapping the edges and brushing on a coat of sealer before applying each additional paper layer. Let the bead dry thoroughly between layers. Repeat this process using the remaining wooden beads.

3 Apply a final coat of sealer to the entire outer surface of the beads. Replace the skewers with clean ones. Let the beads dry thoroughly on the wire rack.

4 Estimate the recipient's wrist measurement, then double it and add 1 inch. Cut a length of elastic cord to that measurement and thread it through the needle. Fold the cord in half and string the beads, alternating the colored-paper beads with the pony beads.

5 Tie the ends of the elastic cord into a tight knot. Trim the cord ends and push the knot into one of the beads so the ends are not showing.

FABRIC LUNCH BAGS

*U*se an easy technique to apply a plastic coating to transform

any piece of fabric into a long-lasting lunch bag. Choose fabric suitable

for each person on your list. Children may enjoy painting a personal

panel to decorate special gifts for their friends.

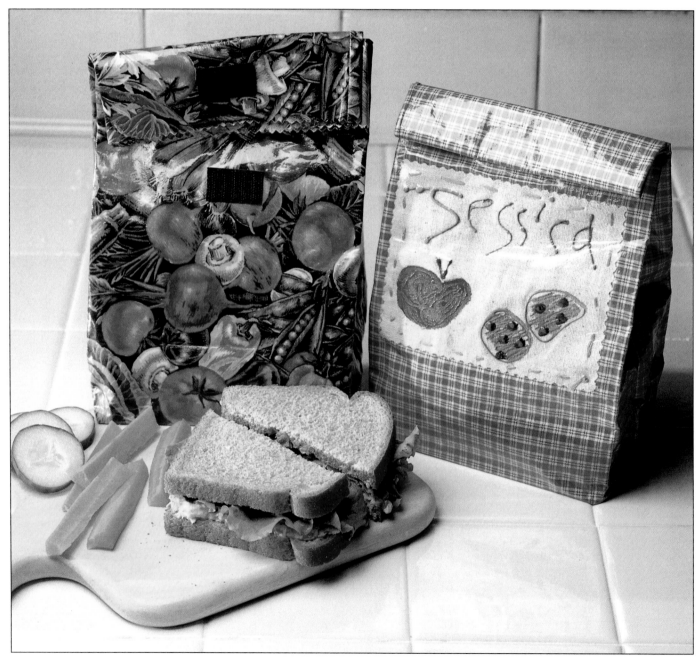

VEGETABLE LUNCH BAG

Size: 3½ × 6 × 11 inches

MATERIALS

❋ Iron
❋ Two 11 × 14-inch pieces of iron-on flexible vinyl, such as Heat n Bond*
❋ Two 12 × 15-inch pieces of fabric
❋ Scissors and pinking shears
❋ Matching sewing thread
❋ Sewing machine
❋ Air-soluble marking pen
❋ 1-inch piece of Velcro
See the "Buyer's Guide" on page 176.

DIRECTIONS

1 Following the manufacturer's directions, fuse each iron-on vinyl piece to the right side of each fabric piece. Trim each piece to 10½ × 13 inches.

2 With right sides facing, use a ½-inch seam allowance to sew the two pieces together along the long sides and narrow bottom, as shown in **Diagram 1.**

Diagram 1

3 Pull a lower corner of the bag out and flatten it to form a point. Using the marking pen, mark a seam 2¼ inches from the point; sew across the marked seam to form the corner, as shown in **Diagram 2.** Repeat to form a corner on the opposite side. Trim off each point about ½ inch from the stitching line.

Diagram 2

4 Use the pinking shears to cut ½ inch off the top edge of the lunch bag for a decorative finish.

5 Fold the bag 1½ inches from the side seam, and sew a narrow and long ⅛ × 2½-inch dart at the fold, as shown in **Diagram 3.** Repeat on the opposite side of the same seam. Then repeat on the other side of the bag. Turn the bag right side out.

Diagram 3

6 Attach the hook (rough) side of the Velcro to the front of the bag, centered 3 inches from the top edge. Attach the loop (fuzzy) side of the Velcro to the back of the bag, centered ¼ inch from the top edge.

CHILD'S LUNCH BAG

Size: 3½ × 6 × 11 inches

MATERIALS

❋ Iron
❋ 5 × 6-inch piece of paper-backed fusible web
❋ 5 × 6-inch piece of muslin
❋ Scissors and pinking shears
❋ Acrylic fabric paints in assorted colors
❋ Small amount of embroidery floss and an embroidery needle
❋ Two 12 × 15-inch pieces of fabric
❋ Two 11 × 14-inch pieces of iron-on vinyl, such as Heat n Bond*
❋ Matching sewing thread
❋ Sewing machine
❋ Air-soluble marking pen
❋ 1-inch piece of Velcro
See the "Buyer's Guide" on page 176.

DIRECTIONS

1 Following the manufacturer's directions, fuse the paper-backed web to the wrong side of the muslin piece. Use the pinking shears to trim the fused muslin piece to 4½ × 5¼ inches.

2 Decorate the muslin piece with the acrylic paints as desired. Use the embroidery floss to sew a line of straight stitching along the outer edges of the piece. Remove the paper backing from the web and fuse the muslin piece to the center of one of the 12 × 15-inch fabric pieces. Following the manufacturer's directions, fuse a vinyl piece to the right side of the fabric, covering the decorated muslin. Fuse the second vinyl piece to the right side of the remaining fabric piece.

3 Follow Steps 2 through 6 of the "Vegetable Lunch Bag" to complete the "Child's Lunch Bag."

SCENTED GIFT SACHETS

*I*n a few minutes, you can turn bits and snips of beautiful craft supplies into inexpensive

yet elegant sachets. Search through your closet for frilly ribbons too short to go around a package,

bits of metallic cord, and pretty artificial flowers and leaves. You can quickly sew up the ribbon pouches,

fill them with fragrant potpourri, and add a trim to create last-minute gifts.

MATERIALS

For all the sachets:
* Scissors
* 20-inch length of 4½- to 5-inch-wide ribbon, fabric, or tulle
* Hand-sewing needle and thread, or sewing machine
* Potpourri
* Rubber band
* Artificial roses, other flowers, buds, and leaves with stems attached
* Scraps of ribbon, cord, and pregathered lace
* Hot glue gun and glue sticks

PREPARING THE BAGS

DIRECTIONS

1 Fold the ribbon or fabric in half lengthwise with right sides facing. Sew the side seams to form a sachet bag, using a ¼-inch seam allowance. Turn the sachet right side out.

2 Stuff the bag about two-thirds full with potpourri. For the tulle sachet, fill the bag with brightly colored potpourri since it will show through the sheer fabric.

3 Fold the top edge in to meet the potpourri and, with your fingers, gather the opening closed. Secure it with a rubber band.

BROCADE SACHET

DIRECTIONS

1 Repeat Steps 1 through 3 under "Preparing the Bags."

2 Group a number of small roses into a nosegay. Add a few leaves around the edges. Twist the stems together to secure. Insert the nosegay into the top opening of the sachet.

3 Tie a knot in each end of a 12-inch-long cord to stop fraying.

4 Knot the cord tightly around the gathers at the neck of the sachet, leaving the ends at different lengths. Using ribbon or a brocade scrap, tie a tiny bow over the cord knot.

TULLE SACHET

DIRECTIONS

1 Repeat Steps 1 through 3 under "Preparing the Bags."

2 Using a ⅜- to ⅝-inch-wide ribbon, make an 11- or 12-loop bow without a center "knot." Each loop should be about 2 to 2½ inches long.

3 Dab hot glue at the center gathers of the bow. Center the bow on the front of the sachet at the gathered neck, pressing glue into the gathers of the sachet.

4 Glue a length of 1½-inch-wide pregathered lace into a circle over the looped ribbon. Arrange several small leaves in the center of the lace and glue them in place. Glue small roses over the leaves.

CLUNY LACE SACHET

DIRECTIONS

1 Repeat Steps 1 through 3 under "Preparing the Bags."

2 Sew lengths of cluny lace together to form a piece about 7 inches square. Gather the top edge of the lace square and hand tack it to the sachet over the rubber band.

3 Fold a 3-yard length of narrow ribbon back and forth to form three 1-yard lengths. Do not cut the ends at this time.

4 Wrap the folded ribbon around the gathers at the neck of the sachet bag and tie it into a bow. Separate the loops of the bows and pull them to different lengths.

5 Cut one set of long loop ends. Glue several rose leaves and buds at the center of the bow. Glue a single large rose in the center of the leaves and buds.

Chapter Four

Gifts for Friends

*T*houghts of friends make the holidays brighter, so rekindle friendships with Christmas gifts you made yourself. This selection of projects includes labors of love like a hearth-warming rag rug and easy-to-craft holiday wreaths to decorate a neighbor's door. You'll also discover a woodland birdhouse and a friendly cross-stitch sampler to keep you in touch with friends near or far. Your friends will cherish these gifts filled with good wishes, glad tidings, and warm sentiments.

HOLIDAY WREATHS

A wreath makes a perfect gift! Coated with glittering glaze, dime-store cookie cutters take on the look of precious metals. Tiny wrapped packages suggest one of the most delightful traditions of the season— gift giving. Use classic colors for the wreath or tailor the colors toward those used in the recipient's home-decorating scheme.

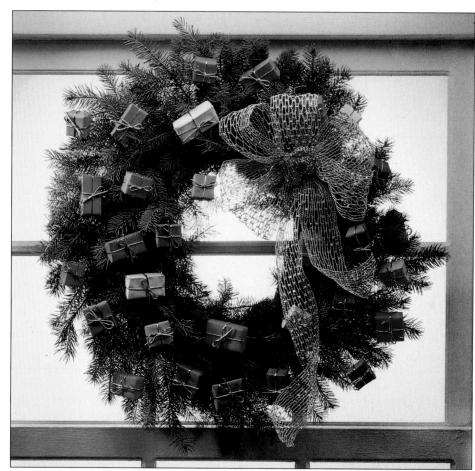

PACKAGE WREATH

Size: 16-inch diameter

MATERIALS

❊ Ruler
❊ Serrated knife
❊ 12 × 36-inch sheet of 1-inch-thick Styrofoam
❊ Scissors for cutting paper
❊ Holiday wrapping papers
❊ Glue stick and fabric glue
❊ 16 yards of gold metallic package cord
❊ Thin florist's wire and wire cutters
❊ 16-inch-diameter wreath
❊ Gold mesh florist's bow

DIRECTIONS

1 Use the serrated knife and ruler to cut the Styrofoam into about 45 blocks for the package shapes. Cut an assortment of blocks in the following sizes: 1½ inches square, 1¾ × 2½ inches, 2 inches square, 1½ × 1¼ inches, and 1¼ × 2¾ inches.

2 Cut the wrapping paper to size, and wrap each Styrofoam block with the paper, using the glue stick to glue the paper edges and corners in place. Do not use tape because it will show.

3 Tie a length of the gold metallic cord around the wrapped package and make a small bow at the top. Place a dab of fabric glue on the ends of the cord to prevent fraying, then dab glue on the knot to secure it.

4 Cut a 6-inch length of wire and wrap the center of it around the cord at the bottom of each package. Use the ends of the wire to attach the packages to the wreath.

5 Attach the bow to the wreath using the ends of the wire.

COOKIE CUTTER WREATH

Size: 16-inch diameter

MATERIALS

✻ 26 assorted cookie cutters
✻ 1-inch-wide foam brush
✻ Assorted metallic paints, such as Plaid Folk Art Metallic Acrylic Paints in Amethyst, Peach Pearl, Rose Shimmer, Champagne, and Aquamarine*
✻ Thick white craft glue
✻ Silver confetti glitter
✻ Thin florist's wire and wire cutters
✻ 16-inch-diameter wreath
✻ White mesh florist's bow

See the "Buyer's Guide" on page 176.

DIRECTIONS

1 Divide the cookie cutters into five groups. Use the foam brush to paint all the surfaces of each group with one of the paint colors; apply at least three coats of paint. Let the paint dry thoroughly.

2 Dilute the glue and apply a thin coat to the inside and outside of each cookie cutter. While the glue is still wet, sprinkle the glitter onto the glued surfaces. Let the glue dry thoroughly, then shake off any excess glitter.

3 Cut an 8-inch length of wire and wrap the center of it around each cookie cutter. Use the ends of the wire to attach the cookie cutters to the wreath. If the cookie cutters do not hang properly with one wire, attach a second wire directly across from the first wire.

4 Attach the bow to the wreath using the ends of the wire.

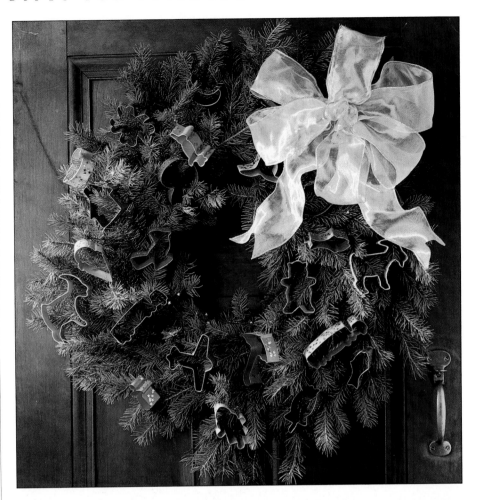

How to Tie a Florist's Bow

You will need about 3 yards of 2- to 3-inch-wide ribbon, weatherproofed if the bow will be outdoors, and a 10-inch length of floral wire.

1. Leaving a tail about 10 inches long, make a 4½- to 5-inch loop. Gather the ends of the loop together tightly. Make another loop opposite the first and gather the ends. The piece will now look like a propeller gathered in the middle. Make a second and third set of loops to either side of the first set, gathering each as before.

2. Bend the floral wire in half and wrap it tightly around the gathered sections of the ribbon. Twist the wires together at the back to hold the ribbon loops in place, but do not trim the wire ends.

3. To form the knot, bring the longer ribbon tail to the front of the bow. Place your thumb over the wire on the front of the bow. Wrap the ribbon over your thumb, gather it up under your thumb, pull the ribbon to the back of the bow, and secure it between the two wire ends. Twist the wire ends tightly again. Adjust the loops evenly around the knot. Trim the ends of the ribbon as desired. Use the ends of the wire to secure the bow to the wreath.

STAMP-DECORATED BOX
AND FRAME

These coordinating desk accessories will add color and a personal note to your friends' home offices or business areas. They may even be a reminder to drop you a line! Buy a packet of canceled foreign stamps in a collectibles store or inexpensive variety packs at a hobby store to add to those saved from your own correspondence.

STAMP FRAME

Size: To fit a 5×7-inch photograph

MATERIALS

❊ Frame with 2-inch-wide molding
  to fit a 5 × 7-inch photograph
❊ Paintbrush
❊ Flat black acrylic paint
❊ Paper
❊ Pencil
❊ Package of canceled postage
  stamps
❊ Small glue brush
❊ Thick white craft glue
❊ Acrylic high-luster varnish

DIRECTIONS

1 If the frame has a glass insert, remove it before proceeding.

2 Paint the front of the frame molding with the black acrylic paint. Let the paint dry thoroughly.

3 With the pencil, outline the frame molding on the piece of paper. Arrange the stamps on this paper-frame outline until you have a pleasing design. Place a triangular stamp at each corner of the frame. Place some stamps at a slant and overlap others.

4 Use the glue brush to apply a coat of glue to the backs of the stamps, then glue them in place on the frame. Glue one stamp at a time, removing it from the planned arrangement and placing it in the same position on the frame. After all the stamps have been glued in place, smooth over the entire surface of the frame with your finger to make sure each stamp adheres completely. Reglue any stamps if necessary. Let the glue dry thoroughly before proceeding.

5 Apply three coats of varnish to seal the front of the frame, allowing each coat to dry thoroughly before applying the next.

6 Reassemble the frame once the varnish is completely dry.

STAMP BOX

Size: 4-inch diameter

MATERIALS

❊ 4-inch-diameter wooden box
  with lid
❊ Pencil
❊ Craft knife
❊ Emery board
❊ Flat black acrylic paint
❊ Paintbrush
❊ Small glue brush
❊ Thick white craft glue
❊ Package of canceled postage
  stamps
❊ Acrylic high-luster varnish

DIRECTIONS

1 With the lid on the box and using a pencil, mark the position of a ⅛ × 1-inch slot for dispensing stamps on the side of the box bottom, as shown in **Diagram 1**. Use the craft knife to cut out the slot, then file the edges of the slot smooth with the emery board.

Diagram 1

2 Paint the outer and inner surfaces of the box bottom and lid with the black acrylic paint. Let the paint dry thoroughly.

3 Use the glue brush to apply a coat of glue to the backs of the stamps. Then glue the stamps to the sides of the box bottom and lid, allow the stamps to extend beyond the box and lid edges by ¼ inch, as shown in **Diagram 2**.

Diagram 2

4 Trim the corners of the stamps and cut V-shaped notches in the extended edges; fold the stamp edges flat onto the top of the lid and the bottom of the box, as shown in **Diagram 3**.

Diagram 3

5 Cover the bottom of the box and the top of the lid with stamps, covering the notched stamp edges as well. Trim off any excess stamp edges. After all the stamps have been glued in place, smooth over the entire surface of the box with your finger to make sure each stamp adheres completely. Reglue any stamps if necessary and let the glue dry. Cut away the stamp material that covers the dispensing slot.

6 Repeat Step 5 of the "Stamp Frame" to finish the box.

TRIMMED PILLOWCASES

Give the gift of one-of-a-kind bed linens. Inspired by Celtic designs, the trim is created with ordinary single-fold bias tape.

White adds an elegant touch to colors while pastels color-keyed to the bedroom add a personal touch to white.

For a really special gift, repeat the design on the top hem of a matching sheet or around the ends of a bolster pillow.

Size: 3⅜-inch-wide tape design

DIRECTIONS

1 Trace the **Celtic Pattern** below, including the dotted lines, onto the lightweight paper.

2 Tape the pattern to a sunny window. Place the hemmed edge of the pillowcase over the pattern and use the water-soluble pen to draw the design lines onto the hem of the pillowcase. Reposition the pillowcase edge to repeat the pattern around the entire edge of the pillowcase, joining the pattern at the dashed lines, as shown in **Diagram 1.**

Diagram 1

3 Mark a second set of design lines on the hemmed edge of the pillowcase, placing them so that the center point of the wide curve of the second set of lines is located at the crossover point of the first set of lines. Repeat the pattern around the entire edge of the pillowcase, joining the pattern at the dashed lines, as shown in **Diagram 2.**

Diagram 2

4 Baste a length of bias tape over one of the design lines, working with one continuous line of the bias tape at a time and easing the tape around the curves so that it lies flat. Overlap the ends of the tape where they meet, turning under ¼ inch on the top tape end and basting it down. Press the tape thoroughly with a steam iron to smooth it into place. Slip stitch the edges of the tape in place.

5 Repeat Step 4 to baste, then slip stitch lengths of the bias tape over the three remaining lines of the design.

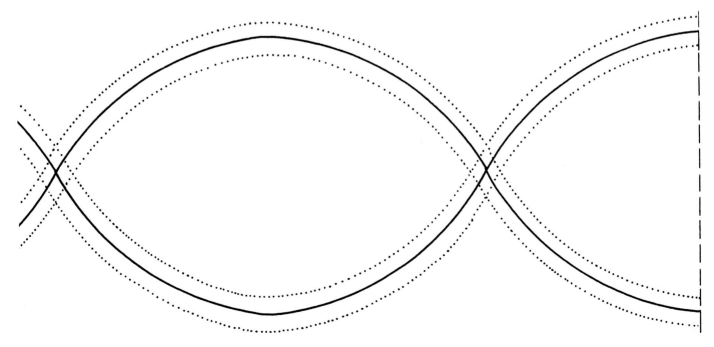

Celtic Pattern

COILED RAG BASKETS

*F*abric strips, a large blunt needle, and stiff coiling are all that's needed to create decorator gifts quickly and easily.

Choose fabrics to complement a certain decor or stick to neutral country colors for a universal appeal.

After a few quick rounds, you'll be surprised at how fast these projects zip along.

Lower right corner of chart

HOLIDAY RAG RUG

*I*magine the look on your friends'
faces when they open this package—
marked "open early"— they'll have a
whole season to enjoy this fabulous rug!
Worked in a very simple variation
of needlepoint, the rug is made of
torn fabric strips. Finish it off with
three rounds of braided strips.

★

Size: 17½ × 29 inches

MATERIALS

❉ Cotton fabrics for the needlepoint center: 1⅛ yards each of
solid ecru and green Christmas
print; ½ yard of red Christmas
print; ¼ yard each of dark brown
and tan; and ⅛ yard each of
bright yellow and bright blue
❉ Cotton fabrics for the braided
rug border: 1 yard each of tan
print and red and green
Christmas prints
❉ Scissors, pencil, ruler, and T-pins
❉ Masking tape
❉ 17½ × 29-inch piece of 3.3 or
3.5-count rug canvas
❉ Large tapestry needle
❉ Rug braiding tools: metal fabric
folding tips, spring clamp or
clothespin, and lacing needle*
❉ Buttonhole twist or strong thread
❉ Medium-size crochet hook

See the "Buyer's Guide" on page 176.

DIRECTIONS

PREPARING THE
FABRIC STRIPS

1 Select cotton or poly/cotton
fabrics and prewash them before
tearing them into strips.

2 To tear the strips, fold the
fabric in half lengthwise and
clip into the folded edge at 1-inch
intervals. Tear the fabric across the
width toward the selvages. You
could also use a rotary cutter or scissors to cut the 1-inch strips. Tear the
fabric strips as you need them since
the remaining fabric will be used for
the braiding. (If you cut the strips
wider than 1 inch, allow for extra
fabric yardage.)

STITCHING THE DESIGN

1 Use the masking tape to tape or
bind the edges of the rug canvas
to prevent raveling. Mark the horizontal and vertical centers of the
canvas. Use these as a reference for
placing the design.

2 Thread a fabric strip onto the
needle. Do not work with too
long a strip or the fabric edges will
become too frayed and worn as the
stitches are worked. To begin, lay
the tail flat on the back of the canvas and stitch over it. To end, run
the strip under four or five stitches.

3 Using the continental stitch,
as shown in the **Continental
Stitch Diagram,** and following the

Holiday Rag Rug Chart below, work the design on the rug canvas. Stitch one row horizontally from right to left and the next row from left to right to achieve the herringbone texture for the background. Follow the chart for color changes, working areas of color one at a time. Stitch the horse and sleigh design first, working from the center out, then stitch the background.

Continental Stitch Diagram

4 Allow enough of the remaining canvas to stitch the four rows of the needlepoint border, then add 1 inch to each edge, and trim the canvas to those dimensions. Fold back the 1-inch hem along the four edges of the canvas piece. Complete the stitching of the border pattern, stitching through both layers of canvas to finish the edge.

BRAIDING THE RUG BORDER

1 Cut or tear the fabrics for the border into 1½-inch-wide strips. Seam the fabric strips together on the bias for a long, continuous strip. You will need to braid about a 2½-yard length of each color.

2 Slide a metal fabric folding tip onto one end of each of three different fabric strips. Using the T-pins, pin this end of the three strips together on the work surface.

3 Using the spring clamp or clothespin to hold the beginning ends of the braid together, braid the strips, sliding the metal tips along to fold the fabric edges.

4 After one braid is completed, sew it around the outer edges of the needlepoint center, stitching through the back of the braid to hide the thread. Ease the braid around each corner so the braid lies flat. Trim the braid ends, leaving 2 to 3 inches to finish. Remove the metal tips. Use the crochet hook to pull the ends of the strips into the braid to complete the weave. Trim any excess strips and sew the ends in place on the wrong side of the braid.

5 Braid two more strips to fit around the edge of the rug, sewing each in turn to the edge and finishing the fabric ends in the same way as the first braid.

Holiday Rag Rug Chart

TWIG-AND-LEAF BIRDHOUSE

*T*his "tweet" little home would make the perfect gift for a bird-watching buddy. You can create

a birdhouse of any size—just collect straight twigs in a variety of lengths. For variety

of texture, shingle the roof with "petals" from dried pinecones.

Size: As purchased

MATERIALS

❋ Sandpaper
❋ Wooden birdhouse, such as Walnut Hollow Farm's Medium Cloud Cabin*
❋ Paintbrush
❋ Redwood brown acrylic paint
❋ Hot glue gun and glue sticks
❋ Assorted twigs (as straight as possible)
❋ Hand pruners or small saw for cutting the twigs
❋ Dried eucalyptus leaves
❋ 2-inch-high craft bird

*See the "Buyer's Guide" on page 176.

DIRECTIONS

1 Lightly sand the birdhouse, if needed, so the paint will adhere better. Apply a coat of paint to all the outer surfaces of the house, including the underside of the roof eaves. Let the paint dry thoroughly.

2 Use the hot glue gun to glue the twigs to the front, back, and sides of the birdhouse as follows: Begin at the base of the house and alternate gluing the twigs around the four sides so they cover the surface; pile them log cabin–style up to the roof, as shown in the **Twig Diagram.** Break or cut the twigs into varying pieces to get lengths as straight as possible, with the twigs extending about ¼ inch from the house corners so the "logs" will overhang at the corners. Cut the twigs to fit around the round opening on the front of the birdhouse.

3 Glue individual eucalyptus leaves in rows to cover the roof. Begin the first row along the lower edge of each side of the roof, overlapping the sides of the leaves slightly. Continue to glue rows of leaves to the roof, lapping each row over the previous row and ending at the peak of the roof.

4 Break or cut a 1½-inch-long twig for the perch. Glue it in place on the front of the birdhouse about 1 inch below the round opening and nestle it between two twigs. Glue the craft bird to the perch.

Twig Diagram

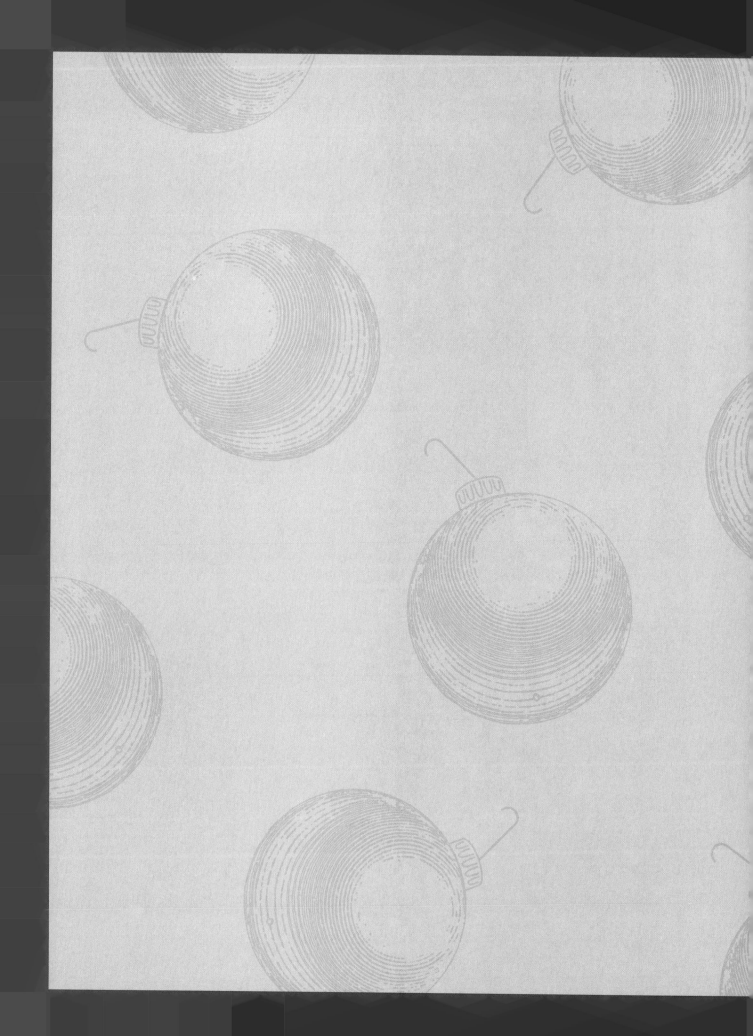

LITTLE GIRL

Size: About 9 inches tall

MATERIALS

❋ Tracing paper
❋ Pencil
❋ Scissors
❋ 12 × 20-inch piece of pink gingham
❋ Water-soluble marking pen
❋ Sewing machine
❋ Matching sewing thread
❋ Polyester fiberfill
❋ Hand-sewing needle
❋ 55 yards of pink yarn
❋ 9-inch-wide piece of cardboard
❋ Pins
❋ Large-eyed needle
❋ 9 × 14-inch piece of floral print
❋ 2 yards of narrow, pink, double-fold bias tape

DIRECTIONS

1 Trace the **Dress** and **Rag Doll Body** patterns on pages 130 and 131 onto the tracing paper. Each pattern includes a ¼-inch seam allowance. Cut out the pattern pieces.

2 Cut two bodies from the pink gingham. Transfer the markings onto the fabric with the water-soluble marking pen. With the right sides facing and using a ¼-inch seam allowance, sew the two body pieces together, leaving an opening for turning. Clip the seam allowance along the curves and turn the body right side out. Stuff the body firmly with the polyester fiberfill and slip stitch the opening closed.

3 To make the little girl's hair, wrap the yarn 100 times around the piece of cardboard. Cut the yarn loops at one end of the cardboard. Open the yarn strands and lay them flat, removing the cardboard and keeping the yarn strands together. Place the strands on a piece of tracing paper, arranging them into a 4-inch-wide hank. To make the part for the hair, use a medium-length straight stitch to machine sew through the center of the yarn hank, as shown in **Diagram 1.** Sew twice along the hair part to secure the yarn strands, then peel the paper away from the yarn.

Diagram 1

4 Pin the hair part along the center of the head with the front of the part about 1 inch down from the head seam. Pin the remainder of the part along the back of the head. Referring to **Diagram 2,** hand sew the hair to the head along the part using a backstitch.

Diagram 2

5 Thread the large-eyed needle with a length of yarn. Sew through the side of the head at the neck and tie the yarn ends around the hair strands to shape a ponytail. Repeat for the ponytail on the other side of the head.

6 Cut two dresses from the floral print. Sew a length of bias tape along the top edge of each piece. With the right sides facing and using a ¼-inch seam allowance, sew one side seam. Bind the entire hem edge of the dress, then sew the remaining side seam, including the hem binding, as shown in **Diagram 3.**

Diagram 3

7 Cut two 19-inch lengths of bias tape for the armholes. Place a mark at the center of each piece. Pin a piece to each armhole edge, aligning each mark with the side seam. Ease the bias tape to fit around the armhole curve at the side seam, as shown in **Diagram 4.** Sew the bias tape to the armhole edge, leaving the ends of the tape free at each end for ties. Place the dress on the doll and tie the tape into a bow at each shoulder.

Diagram 4

LITTLE BOY

Size: About 9 inches tall

MATERIALS

❊ Tracing paper
❊ Pencil
❊ Scissors
❊ 12 × 20-inch piece of blue striped fabric
❊ Water-soluble marking pen
❊ Sewing machine
❊ Matching sewing thread
❊ Polyester fiberfill
❊ Hand-sewing needle
❊ 7 × 10-inch piece of denim
❊ 1½ yards of yellow yarn
❊ 9 × 14-inch piece of purple gingham
❊ 4 feet of narrow, turquoise, double-fold bias tape

DIRECTIONS

1 Replacing the dress with the overall and hat on the opposite page, repeat Step 1 of the "Little Girl" directions on page 129. Repeat Step 2 on page 129 to make the boy's body; use the striped fabric instead of the gingham.

2 Cut two hats from the denim. With the right sides facing and using a ¼-inch seam allowance, sew the curved edges of the hat pieces together. Fold up a ½-inch hem along the bottom edge of the hat and topstitch the hem in place.

3 To make the boy's hair, wrap the yarn ten times around three fingers. Slide the yarn loops off the fingers and position them along the wrong side of the hat front so that the loops are just above the hem. Sew the loops in place with a line of machine stitching, as shown in **Diagram 1**. Turn the hat right

side out and turn up a ¾-inch cuff along the hem edge. Place the hat on the little boy's head and tack it in place. Arrange the hair loops.

Diagram 1

4 Cut two overalls from the purple gingham. Sew a length of bias tape along the top edge of each piece. With right sides facing and using a ¼-inch seam allowance, sew both side seams. Bind the armhole edges in the same way as for the lit-

tle girl's dress. Fold up a ½-inch hem along the bottom edge of each overall leg and topstitch the hems in place. With right sides facing and using a ¼-inch seam allowance, sew the inner leg seam, as shown in **Diagram 2.** Turn right side out. Place the overall on the little boy and tie the bindings in a bow at each shoulder.

Diagram 2

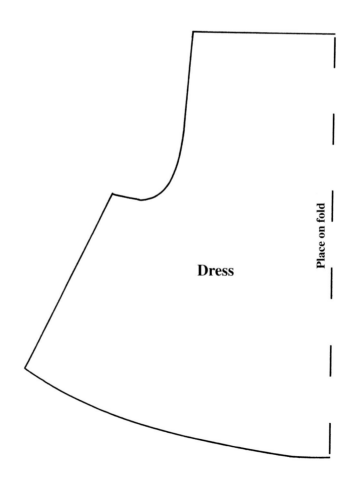

Dress

Place on fold

Overall

Place on fold

Rag Doll Body

Place on fold

Hat

Place on fold

OLD-FASHIONED ROSE AFGHAN

*S*oft colors and a row of floating petals make this little afghan appealing. Older folks will be delighted

that you took the time to crochet this pretty pastel throw. And it's the perfect size

for a lap robe on chilly winter evenings!

Size: About 36 × 46 inches

DIRECTIONS

CHECKING THE GAUGE

To make sure the finished size will be correct, take time to check your gauge. Here the gauge is each square = 5 inches. See "Checking Gauge" on page 61.

CREATING SPECIAL STITCHES

Stitch note: To make 2 double crochet together (2 dc tog): (Yo, pull up a lp in sp, yo and through 2 lps on hook) twice, yo and through 3 lps on hook.

MAKING THE AFGHAN

1 Old-fashioned rose square (make 63): Begin with yellow, chain (ch) 3, then join with a slip stitch (sl st) in the first ch to form a ring.

2 Rnd 1: Ch 3 (counts as 1 double crochet), 1 double crochet (dc) in the ring, (ch 1, 2 dc in the ring) 7 times, ch 1, join in the top of the beginning (beg) ch 3. Cut the yarn.

3 Rnd 2: Join mint in any ch-1 space (sp), ch 1, single crochet (sc) in the same sp, (ch 3, sc in the next ch sp) 7 times, ch 3, join to the first sc. Cut the yarn.

4 Rnd 3: Join periwinkle in any sc, ch 3, in the next stitch (st) work 2 dc, ch 2, 3 dc to make a beg corner cluster, * 3 dc in the next sc to make a single cluster, in the next st work 3 dc, ch 2, 3 dc to make a corner cluster; rep from the * twice more, cluster in the next sc, join to the beg ch 3. Cut the yarn.

5 Rnd 4: Join mint in any corner ch sp, ch 3, beg cluster in the same sp, * single cluster in the sp between the corner cluster and the next single cluster, cluster in the sp between the single cluster and the next corner cluster, corner cluster in the next ch sp; rep from the * twice more, single cluster in each of the last 2 sps between clusters, join to the beg ch 3. Cut the yarn.

6 Rnd 5: Join yellow in any corner ch sp, ch 1,* 3 sc in the corner sp, 1 sc in each of next 12 sts; rep from the * 3 times more, join to the first sc. Cut the yarn.

7 Petals: Join rose in any ch-3 sp of Rnd 2, taking care not to catch the tops of the sts of Rnd 1, ch 3, in same sp work 2 dc tog, ch 3, 1 sc, * all in the next ch sp work 1 sc, 1 dc, 2 dc tog, ch 3, 1 sc to make a single petal; rep from the * 6 times more, work 1 sc in the first ch-3 sp, join to the beg ch 3. Cut the yarn.

ASSEMBLING THE AFGHAN

Use the yellow yarn in the yarn needle to sew the squares together. Referring to the **Assembly Diagram,** sew through the back lps only of the edge sts of each square. Sew the squares into seven strips of nine squares each. Then sew the strips together to join all the squares.

Assembly Diagram

ADDING THE AFGHAN BORDER

1 Border Rnd 1: Join yellow in any outer corner sp of the afghan, * 3 sc in corner sp, sc in each st to next outer corner sp; rep from the * around entire edge of afghan, join to the first sc.

2 Border Rnd 2: * Skip 1 sc, work 5 dc in the next sc, skip 1 sc, sl st in the next sc; rep from the * around, end with sl st in same place as joining sl st of the previous rnd. Cut the yarn and weave in the ends of the yarn.

CHAIR CADDY

*S*titch a gift in bright cheery colors for a friend. Use Velcro to attach this convenient little catchall right to the arm of a chair to keep everything from the TV remote to reading glasses within reach.

---★---

Size: 10 × 11 inches

MATERIALS

❋ ½ yard of fusible web
❋ Scissors, ruler, and iron
❋ Air-soluble marking pen
❋ Two 9 × 12-inch pieces of floral print fabric
❋ Two 11 × 12-inch pieces of gingham fabric
❋ 2 packages of extra-wide double-fold bias tape
❋ Sewing machine
❋ Matching sewing thread
❋ Two 3½ × 23-inch pieces of the same floral print fabric
❋ Two 1-inch-wide buttons
❋ Two 2-inch pieces of Velcro

DIRECTIONS

1 From the fusible web, cut one 9 × 12-inch rectangle and one 11 × 12-inch rectangle. Following the manufacturer's directions, fuse the 9 × 12-inch piece of web to the wrong side of one 9 × 12-inch piece of floral print fabric. Then fuse the 11 × 12-inch piece of web to the wrong side of one piece of gingham fabric. After removing the paper backing, fuse the wrong sides of the corresponding fabric pieces together so the fused piece will be double sided when you are finished.

2 Trim the 11 × 12-inch piece to 10 × 11 inches; this will be the caddy back. Trim the 9 × 12-inch piece to 8 × 11 inches; this will be the caddy pocket.

3 Use the bias tape to bind one long edge of the pocket, carefully topstitching close to the edge of the tape.

4 Referring to **Diagram 1,** press a ¼-inch-deep pleat ½ inch in from the other long edge of the pocket.

Diagram 1

5 Place the pocket on the caddy back, matching the pleated lower and side edges. Bind each side edge of the back with a length of the double-fold bias tape, catching the pocket sides in the binding, as shown in **Diagram 2.**

Diagram 2

6 Taking care not to sew the pleat shut, bind the top and bottom edges of the caddy, tucking under ¼ inch at each end of the bias strips before topstitching the tapes in place, as shown in **Diagram 3.**

Diagram 3

7 Sew a line of stitching on the caddy pocket approximately 4½ inches from the right edge of the caddy to form two pockets, as shown in **Diagram 4.**

Diagram 4

8 Fold a 7-inch piece of bias tape in half lengthwise measuring approximately ½ inch wide. Attach this bias tape piece to the pocket by topstitching it in place, covering the pocket stitching line. Tuck under the ends of the bias tape piece for a professional finish, as shown in **Diagram 5.**

Diagram 5

9 Cut a 3½ × 23-inch section of fusible web. Following the manufacturer's directions, use the web to fuse the two 3½ × 23-inch floral print fabric pieces together so the fused piece will be double sided when you are finished. Trim the strip to measure 2½ inches wide, then cut the strip into two 11-inch lengths, which will be used to make the caddy straps.

10 Place one end of each strap approximately ¾ inch in from the side edge of the caddy front and allow an overlap of 1¼ inches on the top edge of the caddy front. Then sew a button in the center of each of the strap ends. Be sure to tack the straps to the front of the caddy at the same time, as shown in **Diagram 6.**

Diagram 6

11 Fold each of the straps in half toward the back of the caddy. Sew a piece of Velcro to the end of each of the straps and also to the back of the caddy, as shown in **Diagram 7.**

Diagram 7

HIGH-FASHION ACCENTS

Whether you choose to add barrettes, pin backs, or jacket clips, these rose-centered pieces will make perfect gifts. The glorious blooms are created with wired French ribbon and fused pearls. Gathering and folding are the only techniques you have to master to create these lovely roses. Delicate and Victorian-inspired as shown in soft peach, they would be dramatic fashion statements in true red or bright pink.

MATERIALS

For all the floral pieces:
❋ Ruler
❋ Scissors
❋ Low-temperature glue gun and
   glue sticks
❋ Matching sewing thread
❋ Hand-sewing needle

BASIC FLOWER SHAPES

DIRECTIONS

Note: All of the shapes are made with wire-edged ribbon. Use the materials listed under "Gathered Rose Pin" and "Rose Barrette" on the opposite page to craft and customize these basic flower shapes.

MAKING THE GATHERED ROSE

1 Pull about a ½-inch to 1-inch length of wire from both of the edges at one end of the ribbon, as shown in **Diagram 1**.

Diagram 1

2 Twist the ends of the wires together, folding the ribbon in half lengthwise in the process, as shown in **Diagram 2**.

Diagram 2

3 Pull the wires from the opposite end of the ribbon, gently but firmly, to gather the ribbon tightly, as shown in **Diagram 3**.

Diagram 3

4 Twist the wires together at the opposite end and trim away any excess wire. Fold one end of the gathered ribbon over, place the pearl flower stamens on the ribbon fold, and begin wrapping the gathered ribbon around the stamens, as shown in **Diagram 4**.

Diagram 4

5 Continue to gently wrap the gathered ribbon in a loose spiral around the stamens, as shown in

Diagram 5. Tuck the end of the gathered ribbon under the flower and glue it in place.

Diagram 5

MAKING THE FOLDED LEAF

1 Cut a 3-inch length of green ribbon. Mark the middle of the ribbon piece with a pen. Fold each end of the piece over to meet the center mark of the ribbon, as shown in **Diagram 6**.

Diagram 6

2 Make a small pleat on each side of the folded leaf, as shown in **Diagram 7**. Tack the pleat in place at the bottom with two or three small stitches.

Diagram 7

MAKING THE ROSEBUD

1 Fold the ribbon length in half lengthwise. Then wrap one end of the folded ribbon around your forefinger to create a cone, as shown in **Diagram 8.**

Diagram 8

2 Twist the ribbon a half twist and continue to loosely wrap the end around your finger, as shown in **Diagram 9.** Wrap the entire length of ribbon around the finger, twisting the ribbon once or twice with each wrap. Slip the rosebud from the finger and tuck the end of the ribbon into the center cone to finish the bud.

Diagram 9

GATHERED ROSE PIN

Size: 3½ × 5 inches

MATERIALS

❋ 24-inch length of 2¼-inch-wide pale peach wire-edged taffeta ribbon, such as from Offray Ribbon*
❋ 3 clusters of pearl flower stamens
❋ 12-inch length of 1½-inch-wide pale green wire-edged taffeta ribbon, such as from Offray Ribbon*
❋ 2 × 3-inch oval of stencil plastic
❋ 6-inch length of fused pink teardrop pearls
❋ Two 10mm pink pearls
❋ 1½-inch-long pin back
See the "Buyer's Guide" on page 176.

DIRECTIONS

1 Referring to "Basic Flower Shapes" on the opposite page, use the pale peach ribbon to make one gathered rose. Use 3-inch lengths of the pale green ribbon for four folded leaves.

2 Use the glue gun to glue the fused pearls, leaves, and flowers to the plastic oval, referring to the photograph on page 145 for placement. Glue each end of the fused teardrop piece to the oval about 2 inches apart so the teardrops drape below the sides of the oval. Then glue on the leaves, beginning with the end leaves and working toward the center. Glue a cluster of pearl stamens and a round pearl on the leaves at each end of the pin. Glue the gathered rose in the center, and glue the pin back to the other side of the plastic oval.

ROSE BARRETTE

Size: 3 × 6½ inches

MATERIALS

❋ 24-inch length of 2¼-inch-wide wire-edged ribbon in pale peach, such as from Offray Ribbon*
❋ 3 clusters of pearl flower stamens
❋ 1½-inch-wide wire-edged taffeta ribbons: 30-inch length of pale peach and 18-inch length of pale green, such as from Offray Ribbon*
❋ 4½-inch-long French barrette
❋ 1 × 4½-inch rectangle of stencil plastic
❋ 9-inch length of fused pink teardrop pearls
❋ 5-inch length of 1-inch-wide beige grosgrain ribbon, such as from Offray Ribbon*
❋ Two 10mm pink pearls
See the "Buyer's Guide" on page 176.

DIRECTIONS

1 Referring to "Basic Flower Shapes" on the opposite page, use the 24-inch length of 2¼-inch-wide peach ribbon to make one rose; use 5-inch lengths of 1½-inch-wide peach ribbon for six rosebuds. Use 3-inch lengths of the 1½-inch-wide green ribbon for six folded leaves.

2 Glue the stencil plastic to the barrette. Turn the ends of the beige ribbon under and glue it over the plastic. Cut the fused pearl piece in two. Glue one piece on each long side of the ribbon. Working from the ends toward the center, glue three leaves at each end, gluing a cluster of pearl stamens between them. Glue three rosebuds on either side of the center rose, and a round pearl at the center of each rosebud group.

HANDMADE GIFT ENVELOPE

A gift of cash or a gift certificate will be even more appreciated when it is delivered in a handmade envelope. Kids will enjoy making these simple gifts out of decorative paper and holiday shapes.

Size: 4½ × 8½ inches

MATERIALS

❋ 8½ × 11-inch piece of decorative red paper
❋ Ruler
❋ Thick white craft glue
❋ Scissors and pinking shears
❋ Scraps of decorative paper in white, green, black, red, and orange
❋ Tracing paper

DIRECTIONS

1 Fold up 4 inches on one short end of the red paper and glue it at the sides.

2 Mark the center of the extending piece to create the pointed flap. Pink along the glued edges; then pink diagonally from the base of the flap to the center mark at the top edge, then back to the base of the flap on the other side.

3 To make the snowman stamp, cut a 2 × 2½-inch piece of white paper. Cut a 1¾ × 2-inch piece of green paper. Glue the green paper to the center of the white paper. Use the full-size **Snowman Stamp** pattern to trace and cut out a white snowman; a black hat, eyes, and buttons; a red scarf; and an orange carrot nose. Glue the paper shapes to the stamp in the order listed. Fold down the envelope flap and glue the stamp on the point, with 1 inch extending below the flap.

Snowman Stamp

Giving Gift Certificates

❄

It isn't always possible to give a personalized gift to someone you wish to remember. When that happens, think about giving a gift certificate. Many businesses offer them in a wide variety of denominations, and all offer the chance for a special splurge. In addition to the usual stores and services, you might consider giving the following certificates:

❋ **Supermarkets**
❋ **Service stations**
❋ **Retail chains**
❋ **Beauty salons**
❋ **Bike shops**
❋ **Restaurants**

EGGSHELL INLAY DESK SET

*C*reating these very special desk accessories is time-involved and detailed, but the results speak for themselves. The look of a treasured heirloom is captured in this classic craft. If time doesn't permit making the entire set for your employer or coworker, just make the note holder or pencil cup as a small token of friendship.

Size: To fit purchased accessories

*See the "Buyer's Guide" on page 176.

MATERIALS

❋ Eggshells
❋ Large-mouth glass jar with lid
❋ Chlorine bleach
❋ Paper towels
❋ Foam brush
❋ Navy acrylic paint
❋ Desk set pieces: pencil cup, blotter, and memo pad holder, such as canvas ones from Dalee Book Co.*
❋ Masking tape
❋ Ruler
❋ Pencil
❋ Thick white craft glue
❋ Scissors
❋ Single-edged razor blade
❋ Emery boards
❋ Soft cloth
❋ Matte sealer
❋ Cotton swabs
❋ Antique gold decorator's gilt metallic wax

DIRECTIONS

1 Clean the eggshells with warm soapy water and rinse well. Place them in the glass jar and pour in enough bleach to completely cover the eggshells. Place the lid on the container and let the shells soak for two days.

2 After two days, drain off the bleach and thoroughly rinse the shells with water. Set the shells on paper towels to dry. Crack and flatten the shell pieces. Save all the shell pieces; even the smallest piece can be used to fill in a space in the inlay area.

3 Using the foam brush, brush a coat of navy acrylic paint on the outer surfaces of the desk accessories where the inlay is to be placed. Let the paint dry thoroughly before proceeding.

4 Use the masking tape, ruler, and pencil to mark the edges of the gold-color diamond shapes on the desk pieces, as shown in the photograph on page 149. Outline a 1-inch diamond on the pencil cup, three 2-inch diamonds spaced about ⅜ inch apart on each end of the blotter, and one 1-inch diamond on the top of the memo pad holder.

5 Use pieces of shell to fill each diamond shape. Apply a thin coat of glue to the back of a shell piece and press it firmly in place within the taped areas. Allow the shell to crack to create the fine web of cracks that define the technique. Continue to glue shell pieces to fill the taped spaces, shaping the shell edges with a scissors, razor blade, or an emery board as needed to fit the designated spaces. Let the filled diamonds dry thoroughly before you proceed.

6 Use the razor blade to trim the shells along the sides of the diamond for a clean edge. Carefully remove the masking tape.

7 Leaving a ⅛-inch margin around the sides of the diamond shape to allow the background color to show, glue shells to cover the remainder of the surface to be inlaid. Let the edges of the shell pieces extend beyond the edges of the item; they will be trimmed later. Let the item dry overnight.

8 Use a soft cloth to clean off any glue residue from the surface of the shells. Apply a coat of matte sealer and let it dry thoroughly.

9 Use the razor blade or scissors to trim the shell edges that extend beyond the edges of the item. File any rough edges with the emery board. Retouch any navy-painted areas if needed and let the paint dry thoroughly.

10 Apply a second coat of matte sealer.

11 Following the directions from the manufacturer, use a cotton swab to carefully apply the metallic wax to the diamond shapes. Let the wax set for a short time. Apply a third coat of sealer.

CORK FEEDING MATS

A special gift mat will highlight your affection for your kitty or pooch. Since most pets can use your help in the neatness department, these place mats are made from cork to stay put and are large enough to catch inevitable spills. Paint the mats with cute, pet-inspired motifs.

PET COLLAR MAT

Size: 12 × 18 inches

DIRECTIONS

1 Use the craft glue to glue the two pieces of cork together to make a ¼-inch-thick mat.

2 Trace the **Chain Link Pattern** onto the tracing paper. Cut out the shape and use the pencil to outline it on the pop-up sponge. This will be the stamping sponge. Cut out the sponge and wet it so it expands. Squeeze out any excess water.

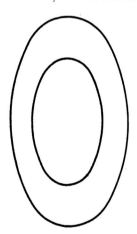

Chain Link Pattern

3 Use the compass to mark a 2½-inch-diameter "dog tag" circle on the cork mat 2 inches from

the center top edge. The tag will connect to the links in the chain.

4 Place the paint on a saucer or palette. Dip the link-shaped sponge in the paint, then press it onto the cork with a light, even pressure. Stamp the chain links ¾ inch from the edge and around all four sides of the mat, overlapping each link about 1 inch, as shown in the photograph on page 151. Use the brush to paint the dog tag silver. Stamp a link to connect each end of the chain to the dog tag.

5 Use the marking pen to outline the dog tag and each chain link, omitting the link outline where it overlaps the connecting link, as shown in the **Link Diagram.** Letter the pet's name in the dog tag.

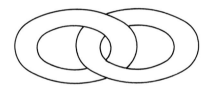

Link Diagram

DOG BONE MAT

Size: 14 × 20 inches

DIRECTIONS

1 Use the craft glue to glue the two cork pieces together to make a ¼-inch-thick mat.

2 Referring to Step 2 of the "Pet Collar Mat" on this page, make a circle and a bone sponge stamp for each paint color.

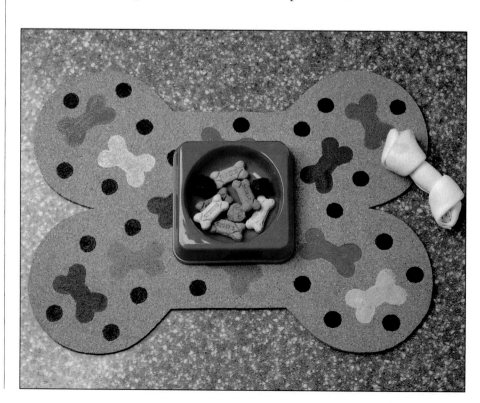

3 Enlarge and trace the **Dog Bone Mat Quarter-Pattern** on page 154 onto a sheet of tracing paper. Cut out the shape and use it to outline the full dog bone shape on the piece of cork, as shown in the **Dog Bone Diagram.** Cut out the mat shape.

Dog Bone Diagram

4 Place the paints on the saucers or palettes. Dip a craft sponge into the acrylic paint, and then press it onto the cork with a light, even pressure. Use a different sponge for each color of paint. Stamp the bones and circles on the mat in a random fashion, as shown in the photograph on the opposite page. Use the paintbrush to fill in any areas skipped by the sponge stamp.

MICE MAT

Size: 10 × 30 inches

MATERIALS

❋ Tracing paper
❋ Pencil
❋ Scissors
❋ Two 11 × 31-inch pieces of ⅛-inch cork
❋ Thick white craft glue
❋ Acrylic paints in bright pink, gray, and black
❋ Saucers or palettes
❋ Paintbrush

DIRECTIONS

1 Enlarge and trace the **Mice Mat Half-Pattern** on page 154 onto the tracing paper. Cut out the shape and use it to outline the two mice shapes on the piece of cork, as shown in the **Mice Diagram.** Using the pencil, mark the eye, nose, whisker, and tail shapes on the cork mat. Trace the **Ear Pattern** on page 154 as a separate pattern. Outline an

ear shape for each mouse on the piece of cork. Cut out the ear shapes.

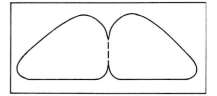

Mice Diagram

2 Use the craft glue to glue the second cork piece to the back of the first cork piece to make a ¼-inch-thick mat. Cut out the mat shape.

3 Place the paints on the saucers or palettes. Use the paintbrush to paint the tails and ears gray, the noses pink, and the eyes and whiskers black. Paint a thin black line between the mouse tails, as shown in the photograph below. Let the paints dry thoroughly.

4 Using the craft glue, glue the ears in place.

Dog Bone Mat Quarter-Pattern

Ear
Pattern

Mice Mat Half-Pattern

1 square = 1 inch

Enlarge 200%

PERSONALIZED PET STOCKINGS

Felt, glue, and fabric paint are all it takes to create special stockings for the furry, four-legged members of the family. Tabby hopes for miles of yarn to play with, while Butch's mind is fixed on treats. You'll have plenty of room for all sorts of toys and temptations in these oversized, easy-to-craft stockings.

CAT STOCKING

Size: 16½ inches long

MATERIALS

❋ Tracing paper
❋ Pencil
❋ Scissors
❋ ½ yard of cream felt and small amounts of red, candy pink, green, medium blue, and orange felt
❋ Thick white craft glue
❋ Dimensional glitter fabric paints in gold, raspberry, blue, orange, and green
❋ Dark green, dimensional shiny fabric paint
❋ Large-eyed embroidery needle
❋ Skein of medium green embroidery floss

DIRECTIONS

1 Enlarge as indicated and then carefully trace the **Stocking, Small Heart, Small Ball, Large Heart, Large Ball,** and **Partial Ball** patterns on page 157. Cut out all of the pattern pieces.

2 From the cream felt, cut two stockings and one 1 × 5-inch piece for the hanging loop. From the red felt, cut eight small hearts and two large hearts. From the pink felt, cut three small hearts and one small ball. From the green felt, cut one partial ball. From the blue and orange felt, cut one large ball of each color.

3 Refer to the **Cat Stocking Placement Diagram** for the position of the appliqué pieces. Use the craft glue to glue the pieces in place on one stocking piece. Let the glue dry thoroughly.

Cat Stocking Placement Diagram

4 Use the matching color dimensional glitter paint to paint the strands of "wound yarn" on each felt ball. Paint six to eight strands in one direction, curving the lines slightly for the wound-yarn effect, as shown in **Diagram 1.** Let the paint dry thoroughly before painting the next group of yarn strands.

Diagram 1

5 Paint the next group of strands in another direction, working over the existing strands as needed. Continue to paint groups of strands until the entire ball is covered, as shown in **Diagram 2.**

Diagram 2

6 With a slightly thinner line of paint, outline the yarn ball. Add the loose yarn tail as a curved line of paint, spreading the paint slightly for a thicker strand.

7 Referring to the photograph on page 155, use the gold paint to outline two of the pink hearts. Paint a scalloped and dotted gold line about 2 inches from the top edge of the stocking. Use the shiny green paint to paint the pet's name across the space above the scalloped line. Use the green glitter paint to highlight the left edge of each letter, as shown in **Diagram 3.** Let the paints dry for 48 hours.

Diagram 3

8 Place the two stocking pieces together with the wrong sides facing. Fold the felt hanging loop in half and insert it between the stocking pieces at the upper back edge. Referring to **Diagram 4,** use a blanket stitch and the embroidery floss to sew the sides and lower edges of the stocking together, catching the hanging loop in the stitching.

Diagram 4

DOG STOCKING

Size: 16½ inches long

MATERIALS

* Tracing paper and pencil
* Scissors
* ½ yard of red felt and small amounts of camel, medium brown, royal blue, green, orange, and bright yellow felt
* Air-soluble marking pen
* Thick white craft glue
* Dimensional glitter fabric paints in gold, blue, and orange
* Large-eyed embroidery needle
* Dimensional shiny fabric paints in green, brown, pink, and pearl
* Skein of pink embroidery floss

DIRECTIONS

1 Enlarge and trace the **Stocking, Dog Bone,** and **Tree Light** patterns on the opposite page. Cut out all the pattern pieces.

2 From the red felt, cut two stockings and one 1 × 5-inch piece for the hanging loop. From the camel felt, cut two dog bones. From the brown felt, cut three dog bones. From the blue, green, and orange felt, cut four tree lights each. From the yellow felt, cut three tree lights.

3 Refer to the **Dog Stocking Placement Diagram** for the position of the appliqué pieces. Use the marking pen to draw the light cord on one stocking piece. Use the craft glue to glue the pieces in place on the stocking piece, arranging the tree lights along the light-cord line. Let the glue dry thoroughly.

Dog Stocking Placement Diagram

4 Use the dimensional glitter or shiny paint to outline the lights and bones. Use the gold paint for the light cord and the pearl paint to paint a wavy line 2 inches from the top edge of the piece. Use the blue glitter paint to paint the pet's name in the space above the wavy line. Use the shiny pink paint to paint a heart behind the pet's name. Let all of the paints dry for 48 hours. Assemble the stocking, referring to Step 8 of the "Cat Stocking" above.

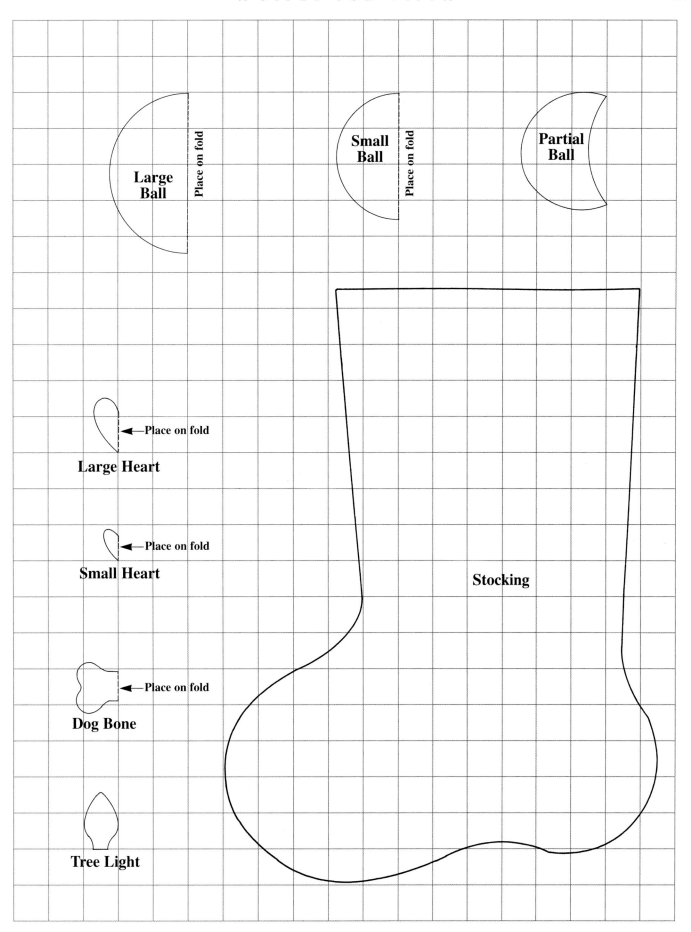

Large Ball

Place on fold

Small Ball

Place on fold

Partial Ball

←Place on fold

Large Heart

←Place on fold

Small Heart

←Place on fold

Dog Bone

Stocking

Tree Light

1 square = 1 inch

Enlarge 266%

Flavor–ite Gifts

*O*ne of the greatest joys of the season is hosting friends and family. We've designed small gifts that can be used as place markers or souvenirs for special occasions. Fill simple herb bags with a mixture of herbs and spices, or craft a fabric game to have at each place setting. Your home-blended bath oils can be formulated to relax or energize. Easy hair scrunchies are ideal grab bag gifts. Involve the family in crafting shapes from polymer clays or in making angels from handkerchiefs as favors.

SWEET HANDKERCHIEF ANGELS

Originally created to keep children quiet during church services, handkerchief dolls required only a few deft twists and a couple of knots. Our angels are beautifully embellished, but the original technique is still apparent. Angels have long been a part of Christmas; let these celestial messengers continue to warm your heart.

★

LACE-WINGED ANGEL

Size: About 9 inches tall

MATERIALS

- ❋ Iron
- ❋ Two 12-inch-square handkerchiefs: 1 white with lace trim and 1 with colored appliqué
- ❋ Small amount of polyester fiberfill
- ❋ White thread
- ❋ Hand-sewing needle
- ❋ 12-inch length of ¼-inch-wide gold braid
- ❋ Small amounts of blue and rose embroidery floss and an embroidery needle
- ❋ Cosmetic blush and cotton swab
- ❋ Short lengths of cotton string or floss in different weights
- ❋ Thick white craft glue
- ❋ Gold metallic thread
- ❋ 12-inch length of gold star garland

DIRECTIONS

1 Press the handkerchiefs to eliminate any creases.

2 Fold the lace-trimmed hankie in half diagonally to form a triangle. Place a small, walnut-sized ball of fiberfill into the center of the folded hankie. Gather the hankie below the ball to shape the angel's head. Then use the white thread to wrap and loosely tie the gathers together. Tie the gold braid around the neck to cover the thread wrap.

3 Fold the appliquéd hankie in half diagonally with the appliqué at the center front. Referring to **Diagram 1,** fold the two side points of this triangle to the back and tack with a few hand stitches. Knot the thread but do not cut it.

Diagram 1

4 Place the folded appliquéd hankie inside the lace-trimmed hankie angel and insert the folded point of the appliquéd hankie in the neck gathers of the angel. Use the thread still attached to the second hankie to tack it under the head, as shown in **Diagram 2.**

Diagram 2

5 Smooth the top hankie. Pull the two side points of the top hankie to the back of the angel, then pinch the ends close to the head to shape the wings, as shown in **Diagram 3.** Then tack the pinched

area of the wings to the back of the angel's head to secure the gathers.

Diagram 3

6 Referring to the photograph on the opposite page, use three strands of floss to embroider the angel's face as follows: Stitching from the back of the head through to the front, work blue French knots for the eyes and two rose straight stitches for the mouth, as shown in the **Stitch Details.** Apply the blush to the cheeks with a cotton swab.

7 Untwist the plies of the cotton string or floss to make tresses of wavy hair. Spread a small amount of craft glue on the top and sides of the angel's head and glue the hair on the head. After the glue has dried, use the gold thread to hand stitch a center "part" in the angel's hair. Twist the star garland into a halo and tack it to the head with gold thread.

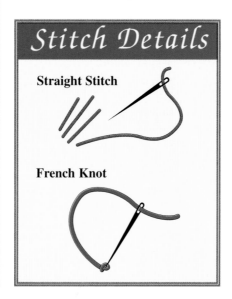

Stitch Details

Straight Stitch

French Knot

Treasuring Yesterday's Hankies

Handkerchief dolls and angels are a delightful way to display fine old handkerchiefs. You will find most vintage handkerchiefs have a main design in one corner; use that area for the front of the angel's "skirt." The lace edging of the handkerchief trims the "hem" of the angel's top. Hide any stained or discolored spots with strategic tucking and stitching—or the addition of a little embroidery.

While handkerchiefs from the early 1900s were usually made of linen fabric, embroidered and lace-trimmed handkerchiefs from the 1930s and 1940s were more frequently made of cotton fabric with brightly colored floral patterns. You will find that each type of handkerchief will produce a beautiful angel with a different look.

How wonderful it would be to present every granddaughter with a pretty little angel made from one of Grandmother's prized handkerchiefs as a family remembrance. Attach a note saying that the recipient should display her angel in a miniature chair, on a keepsake shelf, or floating angelically from nylon fishing line in a china cabinet.

PRINT HANKIE ANGEL

Size: About 9 inches tall

MATERIALS

❋ Two 12-inch-square handkerchiefs: 1 embroidered and lace-trimmed, and 1 floral print
❋ Polyester fiberfill
❋ White thread
❋ Hand-sewing needle
❋ 12-inch length of ⅛-inch-wide green ribbon
❋ Thick white craft glue
❋ Small amounts of dried craft artemisia, tiny acorns, and dried flowers
❋ 6-inch-diameter Battenberg lace doily
❋ 6-inch length of artificial pine branch

DIRECTIONS

1 Repeat Steps 1 through 5 of the "Lace-Winged Angel" on pages 160 and 161 to shape and join the two hankies together; use the embroidered hankie for the head triangle and the floral print for the second hankie. At the neck, tie the ribbon instead of the braid.

2 Twist the tacked "wing" points to form the arms, as shown in the **Arm Diagram,** then pull them to the front and tack the ends of the arms together. Tack the arms to the front of the embroidered hankie.

Arm Diagram

3 Glue on the artemisia for hair, then add acorns and dried flowers for accents, referring to the photograph on page 160.

4 Gather the center of the Battenberg lace doily and pull up the gathers to shape the wings. Tack the wings to the angel's back.

5 Twist the pine branch into a circular halo and tack it to the back of the angel's head.

SUNFLOWER ANGEL

Size: About 9 inches tall

MATERIALS

❋ Two 12-inch-square white handkerchiefs with embroidery
❋ Small amount of polyester fiberfill
❋ Small amount of raffia
❋ Scissors
❋ White thread
❋ Hand-sewing needle
❋ 2 green velvet leaves
❋ Embroidery needle and small amounts of blue and rose embroidery floss
❋ Cosmetic blush and cotton swab
❋ Gold thread
❋ Spanish moss
❋ Thick white craft glue
❋ 1½-inch-diameter silk sunflower

DIRECTIONS

1 Repeat Steps 1 and 2 of the "Lace-Winged Angel" on pages 160 and 161 to form the head; use the raffia instead of the white thread to tie the gathers.

2 Fold the second hankie in half diagonally. Referring to the

Twisting Diagram, pull out the side points and twist to make the arms. Tie 3-inch lengths of raffia at the ends of the arms for "wrists."

Twisting Diagram

3 Cut a small slit just below the head on each side of the first hankie. Slip the second hankie inside the first, then pull the arms through the slits. Pull the points down to form an underskirt.

4 Shape the angel's bodice by wrapping a length of raffia around the body as follows: Beginning at the front of the waist, wrap each raffia end around to the back and then back to the front. Continue wrapping up across the chest and over the shoulders to the back, then around to the front, tying it in the center.

5 Use the white thread to tack the two velvet leaves to the angel's back for wings, slightly angling the leaves, so they show from the front.

6 Repeat Step 6 of the "Lace-Winged Angel" on page 161 to embroider the face of the angel and apply the blush.

7 Cut the gold thread into short lengths. Glue the lengths of thread, along with the moss, onto the angel's head for hair. Cut the stem off the sunflower and glue the flower to the top of the head.

Size: 3½ × 6 inches

MATERIALS

❋ Fabric paints in several shades of green
❋ Saucer or palette
❋ Sprigs of various fresh herbs
❋ Paper towels
❋ 4 × 10-inch piece of tightly woven muslin for each bag
❋ Scissors
❋ Sewing machine
❋ 8-inch length of 1½-inch-wide eyelet lace for each bag
❋ Herb mixture
❋ 10-inch length of ⅛-inch-diameter gold cord for each bag

DIRECTIONS

1 Working with one shade of paint at a time, squirt a small amount of paint onto the saucer or palette and spread it around evenly. Lightly touch the largest sprig into the paint. Press the sprig onto the paper towel to remove the excess paint, then touch it to the muslin, centering it on one-half of the length. Repeat for the other bags. Allow the paint to dry thoroughly.

2 Repeat with the remaining shades of paint and sprigs, arranging them into a pleasing design. Use the darkest paint first, then the lightest, then as desired. Allow the paint to dry thoroughly between each touching.

3 Cut the lace in half. With right sides facing, sew one piece to each short end of the bag. Sew the side seams, using a ¼-inch seam allowance. Clip the corners; trim the seams and turn the bag right side out.

4 Fill the bag two-thirds full with the "Herb Recipe" on this page or your own mixture. Tie the neck closed with a length of gold cord.

Herb Recipe

The herbs used in the featured blend are an approximation of Herbes de Provence. Mix the herb blend in large quantities during the summer when the herbs are inexpensive and easy to come by. You might even grow your own! You will have plenty for gifts and for use throughout the year.

Combine equal parts of dried thyme, rosemary, basil, and marjoram, and blend the mixture evenly. If desired, add a small amount—not more than a quarter of the amount of the other spices—of anise. Store in an airtight container.

PAMPERING BATH OILS

The gift of aromatherapy can reduce stress, revitalize, and refresh. Create bath oils specifically balanced to create energy or calm by blending fragrant oils with herbs, spices, and flowers. These luxurious bath treats are composed of two different types of oil—a base oil for a foundation and a fragrant essential oil.

Size: As desired

MATERIALS

❊ Glass mixing bowl
❊ Spoon
❊ Base oil, such as sweet almond, safflower, sunflower, or soy
❊ Essential oil
❊ Dried herbs, spices, fruits, or flowers, as desired
❊ Decorative glass bottle with a cork stopper
❊ Funnel
❊ Sealing wax
❊ Ribbon or raffia, as desired

DIRECTIONS

1 In the mixing bowl, combine three parts of any base oil with one part of any essential oil to make each bath oil. Stir the mixture thoroughly with a spoon.

2 Place herbs, spices, fruits, or flowers in the glass bottle. Be sure the pieces you have chosen will complement the scent of the selected essential oil.

3 Using the funnel, pour the bath oil into the bottle.

4 Replace the cork stopper and seal with sealing wax, following the manufacturer's directions.

5 Accent the bottle with ribbon or raffia and dried flowers or spice sticks, as desired.

Pleasure Scents

Base oils are light and unobtrusive, supporting the essential oils without confusing or overpowering any of the stronger scents. Essential oils, by comparison, are extracted by a distillation process and embody the very essence of a particular plant. Take the time to search out the true essential oils—the more readily available perfume oils have been greatly diluted and will not produce the desired fragrance strength.

Match your essential oil to the results you desire. Notice that a number of different scents have similar properties. If you wish to blend different essential oils together, try the mixes in small quantities first and allow them to meld for several minutes before sniffing.

❊ **ACHING MUSCLES:** eucalyptus, lavender, and rosemary
❊ **ANTISEPTIC:** eucalyptus, juniper, lavender, peppermint, and tea tree
❊ **REFRESHING:** lemon, lime, peppermint, pine, and spearmint
❊ **RELAXING:** chamomile, clary, cypress, frankincense, lavender, lemon verbena, sandalwood, sassafras, rose, rose geranium, thyme, and vanilla
❊ **SOOTHING:** aloe vera, calendula, catnip, rose, sassafras, tangerine, tansy, and ylang-ylang
❊ **STIMULATING:** bay, hops, jasmine, juniper, lemon balm, marjoram, patchouli, peppermint, rosemary, and rosewood
❊ **UPLIFTING:** bergamot, geranium, jasmine, lemongrass, orange, patchouli, and rosemary

CLAY CHRISTMAS JEWELRY

*S*ome of the simplest polymer-clay techniques have been used to create these timely party favors.

Your guests will love them so much, they'll want to wear their gifts home.

Just be careful—everything looks good enough to eat!

MATERIALS

For all the jewelry:
❋ Craft knife
❋ Clay blocks as indicated for individual projects*
❋ Plastic food-storage bags
❋ White-paper work surface covering for each project
❋ 6-inch length of ½-inch-diameter Plexiglas rod
❋ Ruler
❋ Baking sheet
❋ Wire cooling rack
*See the "Buyer's Guide" on page 176.

DIRECTIONS

CONDITIONING THE CLAY

1 Use the craft knife to cut the clay block into small pieces, as you would dice a vegetable. Knead a few pieces together until soft. (The clay is soft when, after being rolled into a rod, it can be folded in half without cracking.) Add additional pieces of the cut clay into the softened clay and knead until it is incorporated into the mix. Continue adding and softening pieces of clay until the entire block of clay has been softened. Place the clay in a food-storage bag to keep it soft.

2 Repeat the softening process for each color of clay. Store each color in a separate bag until you are ready to work with it.

MAKING THE SHAPES

1 *To make a slab:* Flatten the clay slightly with your fingers, poking the point of the craft knife into any bubbles that appear. Next, place the clay on a paper-covered work surface and use the Plexiglas rod to gently roll out the clay. After a few rolls, lift and turn the slab to keep it

from sticking to the surface and to correct for uneven pressure. Use the ruler to check the thickness of the slab. To make a slab of a certain size, roll the slab to a size slightly larger than the desired finished size. Use a ruler and the craft knife to cut the slab to the correct size and to give it an even edge.

2 *To make a basic rod:* Place the clay on a flat, paper-covered surface and use the palm of the hand to stretch and roll the clay into a rod. Roll from the center out to the ends with light, even pressure. Press the ends in to keep them from narrowing. After a few rolls, lift and turn the rod to keep it from sticking to the work surface. Use a ruler to measure the rod diameter.

3 *To make a triangle rod:* Roll a basic rod following Step 2 above. With the rod placed on a flat, paper-covered surface, squeeze the top between two fingers to shape the top curve of the triangle, as shown in the **Triangle Rod Diagram.** Press from the center out to the ends. Roll the rod onto a flattened side and squeeze the new top edge as before. Roll once more and repeat on the third side for a triangle rod with three equal sides.

Triangle Rod Diagram

4 *To make a candy cane rod:* Roll two or more contrasting color rods, each about ¼-inch diameter. Place the rods together and, holding them at the ends, twist them once or twice to begin spiraling the rods. Roll the rods once or twice to help them mesh, then twist them together a little more. Continue to

twist and roll the rods until the color stripes are as wide as desired. Finish the rod by rolling it until the outer surface is smooth.

CANDY CANES PIN

Size: 5 inches high

MATERIALS

❋ Polymer clays in 58-gram blocks: 1 block each of red and white
❋ 1-inch pin back
❋ ¼ yard of ¼-inch-wide bright green picot-edged ribbon
❋ Strong crafter's glue for metal and china
❋ ½ yard of ⅜-inch-wide gold metallic ribbon

DIRECTIONS

1 Prepare the clay following the directions under "Conditioning the Clay" on this page.

2 Referring to Step 3 under "Making the Shapes" on this page, form eight red and eight white ¼ × 6-inch clay triangle rods.

3 To shape one candy cane, press eight triangle rods (four each of white and red) together with the narrow points in the center and alternating the colors, as shown in the **Candy Cane Diagram.** Roll the candy cane once or twice to round the surface slightly.

Candy Cane Diagram

4 Refer to Step 4 of "Making the Shapes" on page 171 to twist the candy cane. Roll the twisted cane on a flat surface until it is ⅜ inch in diameter. Measuring from the center out, cut it into a 5-inch-long piece. Trim the ends.

5 Repeat Steps 3 and 4 on page 171 with the remaining eight triangle rods to shape a second cane.

6 Bend each cane into a candy-cane shape, as shown in the photograph on page 170. Place one cane on a baking sheet. Position the second cane across the first, pressing them together where they cross.

7 Following the manufacturer's directions, bake the canes and let them cool on a wire rack.

8 Use the crafter's glue to glue the pin back to the bottom cane. Tie the ribbon around the middle of the pin, making a small bow. Trim the ends of the ribbon.

LOLLIPOP PIN

Size: 5½ inches high

MATERIALS

❈ Polymer clays in 58-gram blocks: 1 block each of red, white, and green
❈ Bamboo skewer
❈ Paintbrush
❈ Accent Jewelry Glaze Diamond Bright acrylic glitter glaze*
❈ 1-inch pin back
❈ Strong crafter's glue for metal and china
❈ ½ yard of ⅜-inch-wide picot-edged bright green ribbon
See the "Buyer's Guide" on page 176.

DIRECTIONS

1 Prepare the clay following the directions under "Conditioning the Clay" on page 171.

2 Referring to Step 2 under "Making the Shapes" on page 171, roll one ¼ × 12-inch rod each with the white, green, and red clays. Refer to Step 4 under "Making the Shapes" to twist and roll the three rods together to shape the cane. Roll the twisted cane once or twice to smooth the surface.

3 On a flat surface, roll the twisted cane into a spiral lollipop shape, as shown in the **Lollipop Diagram,** blending the outer end of the cane into the edge of the spiral. Cut a 3-inch length of bamboo skewer. Insert the 3-inch skewer into the side of the clay spiral, pushing it in about 1 inch.

Lollipop Diagram

4 Bake the lollipop and let it cool thoroughly on the wire rack, following the manufacturer's directions for baking.

5 Brush the glitter glaze on the spiral with the paintbrush. Let the glaze dry thoroughly.

6 Use the crafter's glue to glue the pin back in place. Tie the ribbon around the middle of the pin, making a small bow. Trim the ends of the ribbon.

PEPPERMINT CANDY EARRINGS

Size: About 2 inches high

MATERIALS

❈ Polymer clays in 58-gram blocks: 1 block each of red and white
❈ Wire cutters
❈ Jewelry findings: 2 fishhook earring backs, four 7mm jump rings, and 2 eye pins
❈ Needle-nose pliers
❈ ½ yard of ¼-inch-wide picot-edged bright green ribbon

DIRECTIONS

1 Prepare the clay following the directions under "Conditioning the Clay" on page 171.

2 Referring to Step 3 under "Making the Shapes" on page 171, form four ⅜ × 2-inch triangle rods each with the white and red clays. To shape the cane, press the triangle rods together with the narrow points in the center and alternating colors, as shown in the **Candy Cane Diagram** on page 171. Roll the cane on a flat surface until it is about 1 inch in diameter.

3 With the craft knife, carefully cut the cane into two ¼-inch-thick slices.

4 Use the wire cutters to cut two eye pins each ½ inch long. Press one eye pin into the side of each slice. Reshape the slices on a flat surface, if necessary.

5 Following the manufacturer's directions, bake the slices and let them cool on a wire rack.

6 Using the needle-nose pliers, attach a jump ring to each eye pin. Tie a 7-inch length of ribbon to each attached ring, making a small bow. Attach a second jump ring to each of the first rings. Attach a fish-hook to each of the second jump rings. Trim the ends of the ribbon.

STAR NECKLACE

Size: 1 to 2 inches high

MATERIALS

❋ Pencil
❋ Tracing paper
❋ Scissors
❋ One 58-gram block of yellow polymer clay
❋ Bamboo skewer
❋ Assorted colored seed beads
❋ Paintbrush
❋ Accent Jewelry Glaze Diamond Bright acrylic glitter glaze*
❋ Needle-nose pliers
❋ Five 7mm jump rings
❋ 1 yard of black rattail cording
❋ Fabric glue
See the "Buyer's Guide" on page 176.

DIRECTIONS

1 Use the pencil and tracing paper to trace the star patterns on the right. Cut out the shapes and use them for pattern templates.

2 Prepare the clay following the directions under "Conditioning the Clay" on page 171.

3 Referring to Step 1 under "Making the Shapes" on page 171, roll out a ¼-inch-thick clay slab large enough to fit the five star-pattern templates. Then place the templates on the clay slab and use the craft knife to cut out one large star, two medium stars, and two small stars. Use the tip of the knife to cut the clay, pressing the knife straight down into the clay. Do not drag the knife through the clay.

4 Use a skewer to pierce a hole in the top point of each star. Press seed beads into the clay surface of each star.

5 Bake the stars and cool them thoroughly on the wire rack, following the manufacturer's directions for baking.

6 Use the paintbrush to brush the glitter glaze on the stars. Let the glaze dry thoroughly.

7 Using the needle-nose pliers, attach a jump ring in the hole of each star. Fold the rattail cording in half. Pull the folded end of the cording through the jump ring of the large star. Pull the cut ends of the cord through the folded end and tighten to knot the star in the center of the cord, as shown in the **Necklace Diagram.**

Necklace Diagram

8 Knot a medium star onto one end of the cording, spacing this star about 2 inches from the center knot. Knot a small star onto the cording, spacing it about 2 inches from the medium star. Knot the two remaining stars on the other half of the cording to match the first side.

9 Use the ends of the cording to tie the necklace to the desired length. Place a dab of glue on the ends of the cording to prevent fraying, and on each knot to secure it.

Large Star

Medium Star

Small Star

PRINCESS TIC-TAC-TOE GAME

*G*old and velvet and jewels—
all the grown-up trimmings girls
love—make this a pretty favor
for young party guests. The heart-
shaped acrylic gem markers store right
in the drawstring pouch, making this
game a perfect accessory to take
along on overnights and trips
to Grandma's house.

★

Size: 11-inch diameter

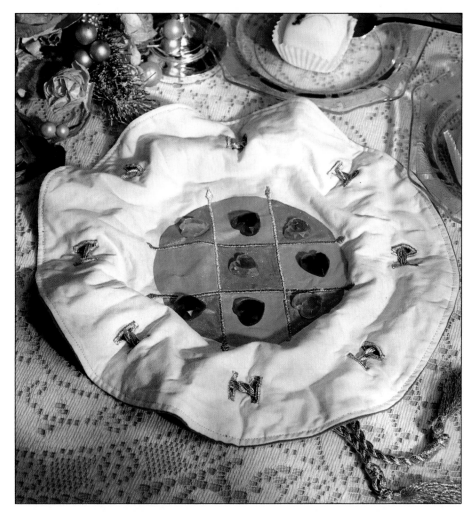

MATERIALS

❈ Compass and paper
❈ 12-inch square each of dark rose velveteen and fine, white cotton
❈ Air-soluble marking pen
❈ Scissors
❈ Pencil
❈ Ruler
❈ Pointed paintbrush
❈ Plum iridescent and white paint, such as Duncan Scribbles fashion paint*
❈ Sewing machine
❈ J. & P. Coats gold metallic machine sewing thread

❈ Matching sewing thread
❈ Hand-sewing needle
❈ 1 yard of ¼-inch-diameter decorative gold cord
❈ Two 2-inch gold tassels or gold thread to make tassels (See "How to Make a Tassel" on the opposite page.)
❈ Thick white craft glue
❈ Large, faceted acrylic rhinestones: 4 each of 2 colors (Here we used Dark Fuschia and Aurora Borealis from The Beadery.*)
See the "Buyer's Guide" on page 176.

DIRECTIONS

1 Using the compass, mark a 12-inch circle on a piece of paper for a pattern. Use this pattern to cut out one circle each from the velveteen and cotton fabrics.

2 Using the compass, mark a 4¾-inch circle on a piece of paper. Cut out the circle and fold it in half, then in half again so it is in quarters. Unfold the paper. Draw a solid line across the circle ¾ inch on both sides of each fold line, as shown in **Diagram 1,** to mark the game's crossbars.

Diagram 1

3 Center the small paper pattern on the large cotton circle and mark the outline of the small circle on the fabric, using the air-soluble marking pen. Also mark the ends of the crossbar lines—where the lines meet the circle's outline—onto the fabric. Remove the paper pattern from the fabric and draw the pattern of crossbar lines on the fabric by connecting the end marks of the crossbar lines, as shown in **Diagram 2.**

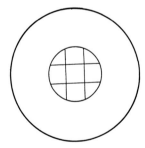

Diagram 2

4 Paint the center square and the four alternate outside spaces of the inner circle with the plum iridescent, as shown in the photograph on the opposite page. Add white to the plum color to make a lighter shade and use it to paint the remaining spaces of the circle. Let the paint dry thoroughly before you proceed.

5 With the metallic sewing thread and sewing machine, stitch a line of narrow satin stitch

along each marked crossbar, widening and narrowing the stitch width at each end to make a diamond shape just outside the circle, as shown in **Diagram 3.**

Diagram 3

6 With right sides facing, and using a ¼-inch seam allowance, sew the cotton and velveteen circles together with matching sewing thread, leaving a small opening for turning. Clip the seam allowance along the curve and turn the circles to the right side. Tuck in the remaining seam allowance and slip stitch the opening closed. Then with matching sewing thread, machine topstitch along the outer edge of the circle.

7 Mark the circle for eight pairs of buttonholes, 1 inch from the outer edge of the fabric and centered above a space on the crossbar circle. Use the metallic thread to sew a pair of ⅝-inch buttonholes at each mark (16 buttonholes in all), spacing each buttonhole in a pair ½ inch apart from the other, as shown in **Diagram 4.**

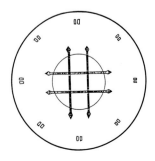

Diagram 4

8 Cut each buttonhole open and lace the gold cord through the pairs of buttonholes on the velveteen side. Tie a tassel 1 inch from each end of the cord. Fold up the end of the cord on itself and glue it in place, as shown in **Diagram 5.**

Diagram 5

9 Referring to **Diagram 6,** wrap metallic gold thread around the cord to cover the end. Trim the length of the cord to fit the circle when it is flat, leaving several inches at the ends for tying. Attach the second tassel to the other end of the cord in the same way.

Diagram 6

10 Use the acrylic rhinestones for playing markers.

How to Make a Tassel

❄

Wrap thread or embroidery floss multiple times around a 2-inch piece of cardboard. Use a length of thread to tie the loops together at one end; cut the loops apart at the other end. Then remove the cardboard and wrap the strands together with another piece of thread, about ½ inch from the tied end. Trim the ends of the tassel even.

BUYER'S GUIDE

We would like to thank the following suppliers for providing us with the products

and support that were instrumental in the completion of this book.

American Art Clay Co., Ltd.
4717 West 16th Street
Indianapolis, IN 46222
Polymer clays, including Fimo and Night Glow

The Beadery
105 Canonchet Road
Hope Valley, RI 02832
Beads and findings

Charles Craft, Inc.
P.O. Box 1049
Laurinburg, NC 28353
Cross-stitch fabrics, including KitchenMates terry towel and Linaida 14-count cross-stitch fabric

Dalee Book Co.
267 Douglass Street
Brooklyn, NY 11217
Canvas-covered stationery accessories

DecoArt
P.O. Box 360
Stanford, KY 40484
Acrylic paints

Delta Technical Coatings
2550 Pellissier Place
Whittier, CA 90601
Paints and finishes, including Ceramcoat Acrylic Paint

Design Originals
2425 Cullen Street
Fort Worth, TX 76107
Rug braiding tools

Duncan Enterprises
5673 East Shields Avenue
Fresno, CA 93727
Paints, including Scribbles fashion paint, dimensional writer, acrylic paint, and textile medium

Fiskars
7811 West Stewart Street
Wausau, WI 54402-8027
Scissors

J. & P. Coats
P.O. Box 27067
Greenville, NC 29616
Yarns and threads, including Red Heart 4-ply Super Saver and Classic 4-ply worsted-weight yarns, and gold metallic thread

Lion Brand Yarn Co.
34 West 15th Street
New York, NY 10011
Yarns, including Wool-Ease Sprinkles worsted-weight yarn and Jiffy yarn

Mundial Inc.
50 Kerry Place
Norwood, MA 02062
Scissors

Nancy's Notions, Ltd.
333 Beichl Avenue
P.O. Box 683
Beaver Dam, WI 53916
Ultrasuede

C. M. Offray & Son
P.O. Box 601
Chester, NJ 07930
Ribbons

Plaid Enterprises
1649 International Boulevard
Norcross, GA 30091
Paints and accessories, including Royal Coat Decoupage Finish acrylic sealer, Mod Podge glue-type finishing sealer, and Metallic Acrylic Paints

Singer Sewing Company
135 Raritan Center Parkway
Edison, NJ 08837
Sewing machines

Therm O Web
770 Glenn Avenue
Wheeling, IL 60090
Heat n Bond vinyl

V.I.P. Fabrics
1412 Broadway
New York, NY 10018
Assorted cotton prints

Walnut Hollow Farm
Route 2
Dodgeville, WI 53533
Birdhouses, including Large Cloud Cabin and Medium Cloud Cabin

Westrim Crafts
9667 Canoga Avenue
Chatsworth, CA 91311
Craft foam sheets